# beginner's guide to
# fly fishing

# beginner's guide to
# fly fishing

## JIM CASADA

BARRON'S

First edition for the United States,
its territories and dependencies, and
Canada published in 2006
by Barron's Educational Series, Inc.

Conceived and created by
Axis Publishing Limited
8c Accommodation Road
London NW11 8ED
www.axispublishing.co.uk

Creative Director: Siân Keogh
Designer: Sean Keogh
Editorial Director: Anne Yelland
Production Manager: Jo Ryan
Photographer: Mike Good

*All inquiries should be addressed to:*
Barron's Educational Series, Inc.
250 Wireless Boulevard
Hauppauge, NY 11788
**www.barronseduc.com**

ISBN-13: 978-0-7641-3250-6
ISBN-10: 0-7641-3250-4

Library of Congress Catalog Card No:
2004117789

NOTE
The opinions and advice expressed in
this book are intended as a guide only.
The publisher and author accept no
responsibility for any injury or loss
sustained as a result of using this book.

Printed and bound in China

9 8 7 6 5 4 3 2 1

# contents

# beginner's guide to fly fishing

# introduction

Fly fishing has a rich, lengthy history dating back many centuries, but until recent decades most Americans harbored real reservations about the sport. That held true not only for the population at large but for many enthusiastic anglers as well. They viewed fly fishing as a sort of special preserve for the affluent, elite, or well connected, and it must be acknowledged that some of those who loved the sport contributed to such misperceptions. There was a distinct tendency, in some quarters, to suggest that the ranks of fly fishermen were reserved solely for a select few. It was considered a "gentleman's" pursuit unsuited for the masses.

Fortunately, a number of factors have combined to change that image, which in truth was never anything but a persistent myth anyway. First and foremost in bringing fly fishing to the attention of the general public and convincing them it was something they would like to do (and could do) was the popular movie *A River Runs Through It*. Based on the book with that title written by Norman Maclean, the film brought all of the grace, beauty, and wonder of fly fishing to the big screen in delightful fashion. After seeing it, viewers readily appreciated the line that opens Maclean's book: "In our family, there was no clear line between religion and fly fishing."

## sport for all

Another factor instrumental in making fly fishing accessible to the average person has been dramatic advances in equipment. Graphite rods have replaced those made of bamboo or fiberglass, silk lines have given way to durable ones requiring little if any care, and the quality of leader material has improved exponentially. Much the same holds true for the many, varied accessories connected with the sport. Best of all, the costs of equipment have fallen. Today you can purchase a perfectly functional, balanced outfit of rod, reel, line, and backing, quite possibly with an instructional video thrown in for good measure, for under $200.

In addition to becoming affordable, fly fishing has in some senses captured the imagination of a nation. Americans correctly view it as a sport that knows no barriers of age, race, sex, or economic background. There are public fishing waters—from municipal ponds in the heart of large urban areas to pristine streams lying "back of beyond" in national parks—that invite angling attention. Fly fishing offers a wonderful escape; a chance, for a few precious hours or days, to leave behind the mad pace of today's society to savor the simple, satisfying pleasures to be found in a line whistling through the air or a rod bent with the gratifying heft of a good fish.

## introducing the tackle

Ample evidence of the sport's emergence into the recreational mainstream is provided by the fact that most of the big mail order sporting goods dealers—Bass Pro Shops, Cabela's, L. L. Bean, Orvis, and others—offer separate catalogs devoted exclusively to fly fishing. Hundreds of other mail and Internet businesses, along with thousands of fly shops, guides, and outfitters, earn a livelihood by catering to those who have discovered fly fishing's many joys.

Even with this changed outlook, many newcomers to fly fishing leave, hopelessly discouraged, after their initial exposure finds them overwhelmed by what seems to be an endless array of complexities—dozens of casting techniques, enough knots to hold Houdini captive,

# introduction continued

tedious terminology with plenty of Latin thrown in the mix, and the like. The purpose of this book, more than anything else, is to break through this barrier of difficulty and reduce the sport to its basic elements. You will discover that when fly fishing is approached in this manner it is simple, not incredibly complicated.

To be sure, as Isaak Walton, the man who sort of ranks as the sport's patron saint remarked almost 400 years ago, "angling may be said to be so like the mathematics that it can never be fully learnt." Yet isn't that what most of us really want in our recreational pursuits—an ongoing challenge that excites and entertains at each new level of mastery? After all, in the school of the outdoors, and certainly in the education of a fly fisherman, there is no graduation day.

## a lifelong journey

There are, instead, many stages in the ongoing evolution of a fly fisherman. Attaining each new plateau of achievement brings its own special rewards and sense of fulfillment. The pages that follow are intended to get you started while offering straightforward, easily understood advice on how to do so. We will cover all the basics— equipment and accessories; the "how to do it" knowledge associated with assembling your outfit, casting, wading, and playing fish; insight on places to fish and how to find competent guides; and much more.

This work is, in short, a step-by-step guide to all the functional aspects of fly fishing with none of the fluff. If some specialized or esoteric aspect of the sport—tying flies, building rods, mastering 50 different knots, or knowing enough entomology to qualify for a Ph.D. in the field—appeals to you, there will be time enough for that further down the angler's road. For now, look at this guide as your textbook, a literary road map showing the way to many years of tight lines and fine times.

1

# gearing up

When it comes to the tools of the fly-fisherman's trade, it all begins with a rod and a reel. In company with the line, leader, and fly, they provide all the items needed to catch a fish. Anything else constitutes an accessory, though as we will see in time, many of these accessories enhance the fly-fishing experience.

# the fly rod

The vast majority of today's fly rods are constructed with blanks made from graphite. Other materials still in use, all of them once popular, are bamboo, fiberglass, and boron. All these materials have some advantages and special appeal, but in almost all cases you should start with a graphite rod. It is strong, light, and has a high degree of elasticity. Also, it dampens (the term used to describe the rod's return to straightness) rapidly after having been flexed.

Fly rods have a number of parts. Here's a brief overview of those parts that provides a basic understanding of the nature of this piece of equipment along with the terminology connected with rods.

Two- and three-piece rods are common, but rods made for air travel or backpacking trips into remote areas will have four or more sections. These are joined together (or mounted) to make the entire rod as it is used in fishing.

The rod has guides, spaced at intervals along its length, designed to direct the line from the base or butt section of the rod to its tip. Most guides are snakelike in shape, but that is not the case with three special guides.

- The keeper guide, located immediately above the handle, is merely a place to hook the fly when the rod is mounted but not in use.
- The top or tip guide is the final one at the rod's end.
- The first guide is sometimes called a butt guide, and it is normally round in shape and commonly has a ceramic interior.

The guides should be well wrapped, smooth to the touch, and spaced fairly close together.

Modern rods are made from graphite, which combines durability and flexibility. Rods are built in two or more interlocking pieces. For backpacking or air travel, a rod may come in as many as seven sections. A good rod is easy to cast, accurate, and powerful, with a comfortable grip.

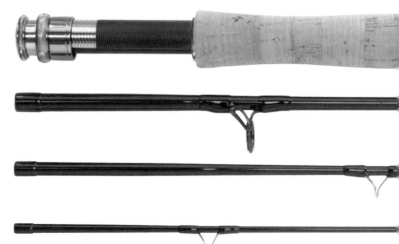

The joint where sections of a fly rod fit together is known as a ferrule. These come in two forms—older rods usually feature metal ferrules, while the blanks for today's graphite rods are designed so sections join at the ferrule without the use of any extra material.

When in use, the fly rod is held by the grip (or handle). Most grips are fashioned from cork, using hollowed-out rings of the light, durable material that are slipped over the end of the rod blank and glued together. They come in a variety of shapes or designs, and finding a grip that feels comfortable in your hand is vitally important to your fishing pleasure.

At the butt end or base of the rod, immediately below the handle, is a reel seat. This is the device used to secure the reel to the rod. Normally sleeves, one fixed and the other moveable, slide over the ends of the reel base. Then the reel is locked tightly in place by rings that screw down. On some rods, particularly lightweight ones, the slides may be all that is used to secure the reel. These are not recommended, as they constantly slip and therefore need to be adjusted.

## THE FLY ROD HAS THREE KEY FUNCTIONS:

**1** It is an extension of the fisherman's arm, and the longer the rod the greater your leverage for casting.

**2** The rod's bend, often described as "flex," acts as a spring to send the fly to its intended destination. In this regard, fly fishing is dramatically different from spin fishing, bait casting, or even use of the old traditional cane pole. With all those rods, it is the weight of the lure or bait that makes the cast possible.

**3** When the cast is complete, the fly rod straightens out and now becomes the means, as with all other types of rods, for setting the hook.

ORVIS CLEARWATER CLASSIC  Length 9' • wt. 3oz. • 5 wt. Line
MID FLEX 7.5

# the fly rod continued

Rods come in many lengths and weights, and your choice really depends on the type of fish you are looking for, and the water and wind conditions you will encounter. Lightweight rods are not suitable for strong winds and heavy waters.

### rod weight

Rods come in a wide variety of weights ranging from 1 to 15. A 1-weight is a virtual fairy wand for use on tiny streams, where short casts are the norm, or when dealing with small fish. By way of contrast, a 15-weight rod is a heavy, powerful piece of equipment used when dealing with large saltwater species such as billfish. To break down rod weights a bit more:

- 1- through 4-weight rods are light and delicate, therefore lending themselves to angling for panfish, small trout, or stream fishing.
- Rods in the 5- through 8-weight class have more backbone. They are suitable for most freshwater species and use in rivers, lakes, or windy

conditions where smaller rods simply won't do the job. Because of their versatility, rods in this weight class are a good choice as a "starter."
- 9-weight or large rods are used primarily in saltwater situations, although they are suitable for freshwater species such as steelhead and salmon.

### rod length

Along with weight considerations, a decision needs to be made on rod length. Standard rod lengths in the popular intermediate weight classes run from 7 to 9 feet (2.1 to 2.75m). There is no best rod length, but some factors to keep in mind in connection with length deserve mention. The

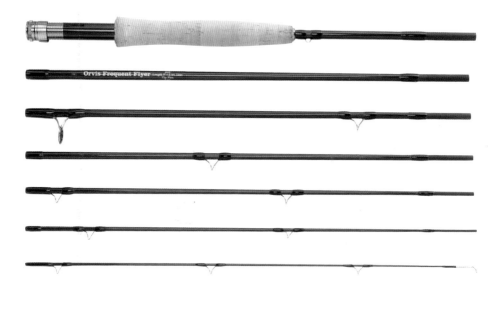

shorter the rod, the more difficult it is to cast efficiently. Longer rods provide a greater mechanical advantage through a longer arc, and for roll casting longer is definitely better. On the other hand, longer rods mean added weight, more air resistance, and, in tight quarters, more difficulty in maneuvering. The important thing is to select a rod length suited to your needs and with which you are comfortable.

For most beginners, an eight-footer (2.5m) is a good selection, and if at all possible, test cast a rod prior to purchasing it. This is not possible with mail order or pre-packaged outfits, but most specialty shops will make arrangements for some testing. They will also offer helpful pointers on rod choice as well, but you will pay more for this service.

## action

Rods also come with many different types of actions. For example, a rod with most of its flex toward the tip is a tip-action rod, while a medium-action rod distributes flex throughout the upper half and a full-action one flexes almost all the way to the handle.

Most off-the-rack rods are medium-action ones, and they are best suited for the novice. In selecting a rod, stability is more important than action. A rod should "dampen," or stop vibrating, quickly after being flexed, and while it is vibrating it should do so in the same plane without any lateral wobbling.

## ROD SELECTOR BY TARGET SPECIES

A simple way to determine the rod you require is to decide the most common waters you are going to fish and the species you are likely to catch, and select a rod to match.

| SPECIES | LINE WT. | ROD LENGTH |
|---|---|---|
| small trout, panfish | 3 | 7ft 6in–8ft (2.3–2.5m) full flex |
| trout (small streams) | 2 | 7ft 6in (2.3m) full flex |
| trout (midsize streams/rivers) | 5 | 8ft 6in (2.6m) mid flex |
| trout large rivers/lakes | 6 | 9ft (2.75m) mid flex |
| smallmouth bass | 6–7 | 8ft 6in (2.6m) tip flex |
| largemouth bass | 8 | 9ft (2.75m) tip flex |
| pike, muskie | 9 | 9ft (2.75m) mid flex |
| steelhead/light salmon | 8–9 | 13ft 6in (4.1m) mid flex |
| heavy salmon | 9–10 | 9ft (2.75m) mid flex |
| bonefish | 8 | 9ft (2.75m) tip flex |
| bluefish/striped bass | 9 | 9ft (2.75m) mid flex |
| tarpon | 11–12 | 9ft (2.75m) tip flex |

# fly reels

Reduced to its basic function, a fly reel is a line-storage mechanism. With smaller freshwater fish, the angler typically plays the fish by controlling line in his off hand (the one not holding the rod). With bigger fish, however, the fish must be played on the reel. That is when drag enters the equation. As is the case with rods, you need to consider the type of fish you will be going after and get a reel suited to it.

The first factor in choosing a reel is weight. It must balance with your rod, and for that reason reels come with weights just like rods do. For example, you should outfit a 7-weight rod with a 7-weight reel. Many reels, especially inexpensive ones, may actually be marked as suitable for two or even three rod weights, such as 5/6 or 5/6/7.

## reel action

Most fly-fishing reels are of the single-action type. That is to say, one turn of the reel handle will turn the spool of the reel once. This is in marked contrast to many bait- and spin-casting reels, where a gear mechanism gives more than one spool revolution for a full turn of the handle. At one time automatic reels, which retrieved line through use of a lever-activated spring, also saw wide use in fly fishing. However, they are heavy, causing rod imbalance, lack good drag systems, and tear up easily. They are not recommended.

Rod, reel, and line are the core pieces of equipment you will buy. Assess the whole rig for balance, ease of use, and comfort before you make a purchase.

## spools

Most good fly reels have removable spools. This is a desirable feature, and when buying a reel it is a good idea to acquire one or two extra spools. These can carry different types of line, which equip the angler to handle most fishing situations. Another useful feature is a reel with an exposed-rim spool. This lets the angler add extra drag by placing the palm of his hand against the spool's rim when a fish is taking out line, and "palming the reel" is particularly important when dealing with big, powerful fish.

Large fish place a premium on a reliable drag system. You need one that works smoothly under pressure while exerting solid, steady resistance during the fight to land a fish. It should never allow spool overrun. The "guts" of a reel provides the drag, usually with a ratchet-and-pawl system or with disks. The latter are pads that place pressure, which can be adjusted to the appropriate degree of tension, directly on the reel spool. Ratchet-and-pawl systems are designed to maintain light tension when line is being pulled off the reel. They are best for most freshwater fishing situations.

One other reel feature is the option of either-hand retrieve, meaning you can switch from right-hand to left-hand reeling with ease. In some cases the changeover can be a bit complicated thanks to the need to remove and flip over pawls. Make sure you understand how the change is done, and for beginners it is wise to specify whether you want to reel with your right hand or your left.

Finally, in selecting a reel, obviously you want a reel base that fits snugly into the seat of your rod.

The table below summarizes the key points to keep in mind when selecting your rod and reel.

## THE REEL CRITERIA

Before buying a reel there are several points to consider, in terms of usability for the type of fishing you will be doing. The rod and reel are the most significant pieces of equipment you will buy, from the standpoints of function and expense.

**1 reel capacity** How much line and backing a reel will hold, and the size of its base, are important. You want a reel that will hold any type of line you decide to use (see fly lines, pp. 20–23) along with the desirable amount of backing. The reel should be reasonably full but not overloaded when all the line is reeled in.

**2 rod balance** Rod and reel should be compatible for a balanced outfit. If you are uncertain about balance, put the reel on the rod, string it up with line, and check the balance. If the pivot point is at, or very close to, the grip, the balance is correct.

**3 interchangeable spools** A reel with a system for easy spool removal allows you to carry several different line weights at any time to meet changing weather conditions, or gives you a choice of quarries when the one you intended to fish will not bite.

**4 drag system** The drag system provides tension on the line. Tension regulates the ease with which fish pull line from the reel. A large fish can strip line fast, making a good drag system vital. For small fish, which are unlikely to pull out much line, your drag system is less important. There are basically two types of drag system: ratchet and pawl and disk drag (see p.19).

# fly reels continued

## beginner ▸▸

An entry level reel in terms of price and function, this features an interchangeable spool, so that line weights can be changed immediately to suit the prevailing quarry and conditions. It is also corrosion resistant.

## ◂◂ strong

A good combination of price and reliability, this reel is drilled from solid aluminum, making it lightweight and exceptionally strong, as well as highly resistant to corrosion. This also features an interchangeable spool.

## metal ▸▸

This cast metal frame has interchangeable plastic cartridges so that line can be changed immediately. This is another good reel for beginners, inexpensive yet strong and reliable.

# ◄◄ extra light

This extra light reel has a large line capacity for heavy weight line, making it ideal for big game fish. It has an easy left- to right-hand switch. Smooth and reliable, it is hardwearing and almost maintenance free.

## DRAG SYSTEMS

Most of the time, you will play smaller fish on the line. However, the downsides of this are that the fish can break the line, and you might not be able to land the fish. This is when your reel needs a good drag system.

The drag system applies tension to the line. The majority of reels suitable for beginners and for most fishing situations feature a ratchet-and-pawl system. This allows a smooth release of line. A ratchet pushes the pawl into a gear on the reel spool to create drag. Some models use a knob to increase or decrease drag tension, others feature a fixed drag tension.

This drag system is best suited for lighter fishing, such as trout and panfish.For larger fish that can strip out large quantities of line at a time, a disk-drag system, in which a pad applies tension directly to the reel spool is usually more effective.

# fly lines

The technological advances that have revolutionized fly rods have also seen dramatic changes in fly lines. Today's lines perform almost flawlessly (they still require user ability, of course) and are virtually maintenance-free. When selecting a line, keep squarely in mind its intended function. The line is the tool that delivers the fly, as opposed to the weight of the lure. Different situations and types of fishing require different lines, but there's one constant that never changes. As is the case with reels, you must always match your line to the weight of your rod. A balanced outfit works well, and without one you are in a world of trouble. Even the most accomplished caster handling a badly mismatched outfit will struggle as if he was whipping a rope with a hoe handle!

There are four basic characteristics to be considered in selecting a fly line:

■ weight—to match your rod and reel;
■ type of taper;
■ color; and
■ whether the line floats or sinks, and if the latter, at what rate.

Wind, water depth, and species of fish are also part of the selection process. Do not think, however, that you need several different lines for each rod. A fly-fishing beginner can manage with one or two lines.

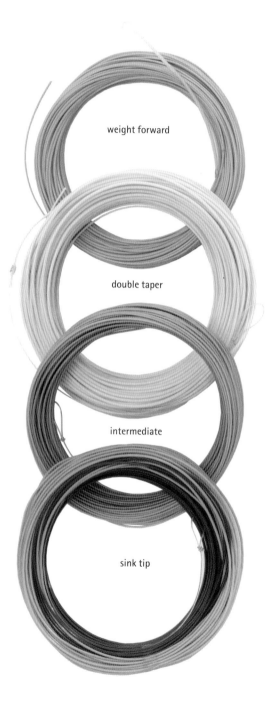

weight forward

double taper

intermediate

sink tip

## line weight

Fly-fishing lines were once categorized by diameter, instead of weight, and that made for confusion. Even today, when weight is the determining factor, line descriptions can be mystifying. How is the beginner to know what DT-4-5-F means? It is the symbolism for a double-tapered, floating line for a 4- or 5-weight rod, but that's not readily obvious. If uncertain, just ask; and if you buy a complete outfit as a kit, the line weight will be appropriate.

## shape

Along with weight, you should be aware of the various shapes used in fly-line manufacture.

■ Level lines are precisely what they say—the same size from one end to the other. They are the least expensive type of line, thanks to being easy to make. However, they do not cast well, and where delicacy of the cast makes a difference, level lines are a liability. They are acceptable for panfishing, but even there they are not recommended.

■ A double-tapered line is the best choice for the novice. While double tapers are not quite as popular as they were a generation ago, they have one quality that really recommends them to the budget-conscious angler; they will last twice

## FLY-LINE PROFILES

**1** LEVEL

**2** DOUBLE-TAPER

**3** WEIGHT FORWARD

**4** QUICK SINK TIP

**5** SHOOTING TAPER—BUG BELLY

# fly lines continued

as long for most types of fishing. That's because when the end with which you have been fishing begins to show signs of wear or develops cracks in the line coating, you can turn it around and fish with the other end. Most lines range in length between 75 and 100 feet (23–31m), but commonly only the first 40 or 50 feet (12–15m) see much usage. That's especially the case with rods in the lower weight classes, and only the expert can cast all of a 100-foot (31m) line with accuracy and ease. A double-tapered line works nicely when false casting, roll casting, or endeavoring to present a fly with delicacy. Make this your first line if at all possible.

■ The two other types of lines are weight-forward and shooting taper. The latter is sometimes called "bug taper" or "long belly." These are

## QUICK GUIDE—WHICH FLY LINE?

Picking the right line for the job can be confusing, as there are many factors to take into account. If you are fishing with dry flies you will only need a floating line, but the choices when nymph or lure fishing are infinite. Here is a basic guide to making the right decision and getting to the fish.

| WATER TYPE | LINE TYPE | COLOR |
|---|---|---|
| DEEP LAKES AND RESERVOIRS | FAST SINKING quickly gets to where the fish are | use darker colors, the fish are less likely to be spooked by them |
| RIVERS, FAST WATER | SINK TIP gets nymphs, wet flies, or streamers down quite quickly into deep holes or fast water | sink tips are generally darker in color, with the floating part lighter |
| LAKES WITH A LOT OF WEED | INTERMEDIATE takes the fly down beneath the surface but keeps it above the weed | any sub-surface line should be darker in color, less visible to the fish |
| SHALLOW STREAMS AND RIVERS | FLOATING the floating line is also a good all-rounder, ideal for the beginner as it is easier to cast | most are bright colors, but this can be a problem in clear waters or where fish are very spooky |
| SALTWATER | FAST SINKING gets the fly down to the fish as quickly as possible | the brighter color lines will help with visibility |

specialized lines designed for longer casts or to pull a big bass bug or saltwater fly through the air in efficient fashion.

## color

Give some thought to line color. Fluorescent orange and bright yellow lines have their virtues—they are a delight to photographers and make it easy to see the line when nymph streamer fishing. Generally speaking, though, you will be better served by lines in earth tones—brown, gray, or dull green—because they are less likely to be spotted by fish.

## sinking and floating lines

When fly lines land on the water, they do one of two things—float or sink. For dry fly fishing as well as all types of techniques in shallow water or moderate currents, you need a floating line. Today we have floating lines that ride high in the water while requiring no dressing or special treatment other than occasional cleaning. Sinking lines, which come in many forms, from sinking tips to those with lead cores, can be used when your fly is below the surface. They come into their own:

- in powerful rivers where it is important to get the fly down deep;
- in still-water situations demanding that you get the fly several feet down; and
- on the relatively rare occasions when the fly fisherman trolls from a canoe.

All things considered though, it is best to start out with a floating line. You can always use split shot or a weighted fly to get down in the depths.

As is the case with rods and reels, line weight is indicated by a simple numbering system. Once you select a rod, its weight tells you the required line weight, and matching the line and rod, along with the reel, provides the balance that is so essential for casting.

## LINE CARE

Caring for your lines is simple and straightforward. Occasional cleaning with mild soap and a wet cloth is recommended, and this is particularly important if you have fished in a location with moss, algae, or scum present. Avoid, at all costs, letting the line come in contact with solvents such as insect repellent or suntan lotion. Some of these can literally "eat" up an expensive line. Likewise, do not store lines for any length of time in direct sunlight, damp conditions, or high heat. All will appreciably shorten line life. With minimal care and some common sense, you should get several seasons out of a line; and don't forget that a good line, like a good rod, lets you cast better. Better casts translate to greater likelihood of catching fish, and that is everyone's ultimate goal.

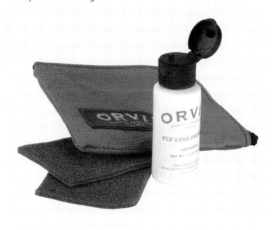

# leaders and tippets

*Cutting your own tippets and leaders from a roll of fluorocarbon monofilament is more cost-effective than buying ready made.*

The terminal tackle in fly fishing is appropriately called a leader, because the slender piece of monofilament connecting the line to the fly is the "leading" element in the cast. Sometimes the leader is completed or tipped with a short strand of material; hence, the word

tippet for the final section of leader where the fly is attached. Leaders vary quite a bit in length and strength, depending on the angler's quarry and conditions. However, their purpose is always the same; namely, to present the fly in a realistic, undetectable fashion. Accordingly, small diameter, minimal visibility, and suitable strength are key criteria for leaders.

Today, almost all leader material is made from nylon monofilament or some related synthetic. Improved technology has seen a pronounced move toward increasing leader strength, in relation to diameter, along with reduced visibility.

There are two types of leaders—knotted and knotless. Both taper down from a thick section of monofilament that is fairly close to the size of the line it joins to a much smaller diameter where the fly is tied. The taper lends itself to a smooth turnover in casting, which means that the fly is the last thing to touch the water in a well-executed cast.

## knotless leaders

Knotless or single-strand leaders are readily available in stores selling fly fishing equipment. They normally come in three lengths—7.5, 9, and 12 feet (2.3, 2.75, and 3.7m). That can be a problem when you face a situation requiring, for example, an exceptionally lengthy leader. Another problem with knotless leaders is that, after tying on and removing a few flies, you must add a tippet to them or else you will be too far up the taper. These disadvantages notwithstanding, most fishermen rely on knotless leaders, and they are the best "starter" choice.

## knotted leaders

Most fly fishermen, as they progress, eventually opt to use knotted leaders. One big plus is that they save money. Purchase several spools of good leader material in varying sizes, achieve solid mastery of the blood knot (see p. 44), and you are set to produce your own leaders. You can tie up dozens of knotted leaders for the same amount of money you would spend buying half a dozen knotless ones. Another advantage is that you can make them as long and strong as you want; and by following a simple 60–20–20 formula, you can tie up functional leaders of any desired length.

The formula places 60 percent of the leader length in the butt (end attaching to the line), 20 percent in the taper, and 20 percent in the tippet. The table below gives detailed formulas for three 12-foot (3.7m) leaders, all meeting the formula but tapering to different tippets and containing different elements.

Use this table as a guide to putting line and leader together. The formula can be applied to any line.

## 12-FOOT LEADERS

| LEADER 1 | LEADER 2 | LEADER 3 |
|---|---|---|
| **BUTT SECTION** | | |
| 36in. (92cm) of 25-lb. test | 36 in. (92cm) of 25-lb. test | 28in. (71cm) of 25-lb. test |
| 24in. (61cm) of 20-lb. test | 24 in. (61cm) of 20-lb. test | 18in. (46cm) of 20-lb. test |
| 16in. (41cm) of 15-lb. test | 20 in. (50cm) of 15-lb. test | 16in. (41cm) of 15-lb. test |
| **TAPER SECTION** | | |
| 12in. (30cm) of 10-lb. test | 12in. (30cm) of 10-lb. test | 14in. (36cm) of 10-lb. test |
| 10 in. (25cm) of 8-lb. test | 12in. (30cm) of 8-lb. test | 12in. (30cm) of 8-lb. test |
| 7in. (18cm) of 6-lb. test | 12in. (30cm) of 6-lb. test | 8in. (20cm) of 6-lb. test |
| 7in. (18cm) of 4-lb. test | 8in. (20cm) of 4-lb. test | 8in. (20cm) of 2-lb. test |
| **TIPPET** | | |
| 32in. (81cm) of 2-lb. test | 28in. (71cm) of 4-lb. test | 36in. (92cm) of 1-lb. test |

In the final analysis, selecting the appropriate leader is a matter of personal choice. You will need to use a leader you can cast easily and that meets prevailing conditions such as wind, water clarity, and what you need in terms of tippet for the species involved.

# flies—the final essential

The word "flies" implies fishing with insect imitations. To an appreciable degree this is true, but in an angling context flies also imitate a wide range of non-insect food items—minnows; crabs, crayfish, and other crustaceans; lizards; worms; frogs; small snakes; and the like. There are thousands, perhaps tens of thousands, of fly patterns, and innovative fly tiers constantly create new ones.

A fly box is not essential, but it is a good way to organize and protect your flies, and means whatever pattern you need for your quarry is at hand.

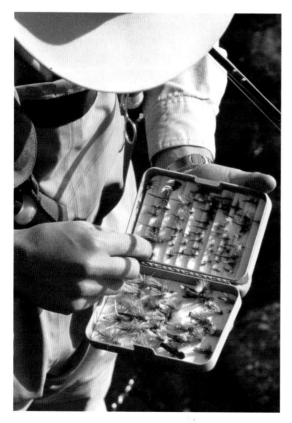

Flies come in two basic categories—attractors and imitators.

- Attractors draw the attention of fish, even though they may not imitate a specific food item.
- Imitators look like food the fish regularly eats.

### attractor flies

Attractor flies work in any of several ways. They may not closely resemble a specific insect, but in shape and size they have the general form of a number of insects. The classic example is the fly pattern known as the Royal Wulff, named for the famous fly fisherman, Lee Wulff. The most popular of all dry flies, it has a "buggy" shape to attract fish (and a showy appearance, with white wings and a red body). With this pattern, as is the case with most attractors, shape is the key factor. The fish sees the fly, reacts to the fact that it looks like things the fish is used to eating, and instinctively eats it.

Attractors can also appeal to fish through motion or sound, such as a popping bug skittering and gurgling on the surface of a pond or the body of a streamer pulsating like a minnow breathing as it is worked through the water with jerks and twitches.

### imitator flies

In contrast to attractors, imitators draw attention because fish react to them as something that appears regularly on the menu. The idea is to offer a fly pattern that imitates—to the greatest degree possible (in size, shape, color, and the like)—a real insect.

## on or below the surface

Both attractors and imitators are always fished in one of two fashions—on the surface or beneath it. Most popular game fish obtain the vast majority of their food, 90 percent or more, beneath the surface. Even trout, noted surface feeders, obtain at least 75 percent of their sustenance underwater. There's an obvious message here. Fish with flies intended to be used in the water, not on it, and you greatly increase the likelihood of success. Yet most of us feel a great

affinity for dry fly fishing. There's something about seeing a trout take a dry fly in a lovely head-and-shoulders rise or watching a chunky largemouth bass inhale a popper that produces a special thrill. Nor should the persistent myth—and it is nothing but a myth—suggesting that true sportsmen rely exclusively on dry flies be overlooked. Skilled nymph fishing requires at least as much mastery as successful dry fly fishing; and there's no doubt that day in and day out, an accomplished nymph fisherman will catch more fish.

Dry flies, and their floating first cousins, poppers, have a special appeal to those just getting started. They let the angler see the strike when it occurs, and this makes hook setting

## ANATOMY OF A NYMPH

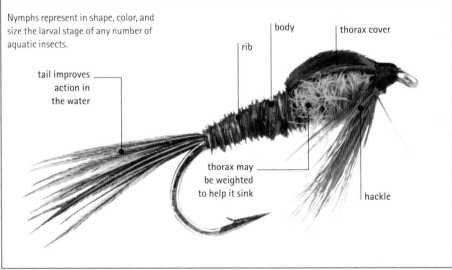

Nymphs represent in shape, color, and size the larval stage of any number of aquatic insects.

tail improves action in the water

rib

body

thorax cover

thorax may be weighted to help it sink

hackle

# flies—the final essential continued

easier. Delicate hits of sub-surface flies can be difficult to detect. Also, in moving water, telling whether a fly is moving naturally (as opposed to "dragging" in an unnatural fashion) is easier when the fly is on the surface.

Use of dry flies is an effective way to catch a wide variety of both freshwater and saltwater species. There are two basic types of dry fly fishing—casting to visible fish or casting "blind." When casting to a fish you have seen, either thanks to a rise or through spotting it in the water, you try to place a fly in the immediate area without spooking it.

Casting to invisible fish, on the other hand, involves placing the fly in promising locations or ones that previous experience has suggested might produce strikes. Over time, an alert angler develops a real "feel" for the sort of places he is likely to locate fish.

When fishing sub-surface flies, the sport takes on a different dimension because the action occurs out of sight

(there are exceptions in clear, shallow water conditions). Touch, instinct, observation, and experience are prominent in this aspect of fly fishing. An overview of the types of sub-surface flies should make matters clearer.

Wet flies somehow seem to be passé today, but they are the oldest of all artificials. Moreover, they still work well, and every fly fisherman should understand how to use them. There are two styles of wet flies:

■ soft hackle wrapped around the top part of the hook shank, which is covered with some sort of material
■ a wing stretching along the top of the hook shank (known as a down-wing fly).

Wet flies are often fished in tandem (two or three flies attached to a single leader), with one of the flies being bright colored to attract attention. Common approaches to fishing wet flies include letting them "dead drift" with the current, and retrieving with a steady repetitive motion, occasionally interspersed with twitches or stops.

## streamers

Occasionally called bucktails because of the material commonly used to tie them, streamers imitate minnows and, occasionally, eels or lizards. All flies of this type come in a slender, streamlined profile comparable to a minnow, and most are tied on long shank hooks. In a sense, streamers are nothing more

Surface flies may make some noise to attract fish. This pattern "pops" as it moves across the water. A couple of twitches and a wait may be all you need to get a strike.

than long, large wet flies, although they are fished in different fashion. In moving water, they are cast down and across the current, and then retrieved as the current carries the line and fly downstream. Strikes frequently occur as the line straightens out and the fly begins to rise toward the surface, as if it was about to escape. One advantage of streamer fishing, especially in moving water, is that strikes are easy to detect. In fact, fish often hook themselves.

Dry flies sit on the surface of the water, and may be made from water-resistant material to increase buoyancy. Many are designed to imitate a specific insect species.

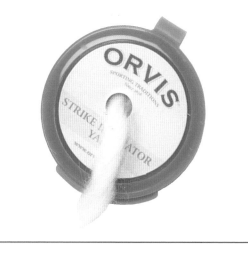

## nymphs

When it comes to all-out fish-catching effectiveness, nymphs garner top ratings. A nymph is a fly tied to imitate the larval form of some insect that deposits its eggs in the water. The diet of many species of fish relies heavily on this phase of insect life. Nymphs also imitate other fish foodstuffs such as scuds (freshwater shrimp).

While nymphs are plentiful and readily eaten by fish, mastering nymph fishing is the fly fisherman's ultimate challenge. This is thanks in considerable measure to the difficulty of detecting strikes.

Methods for working nymphs in the water are similar to those for other underwater flies—dead drift, stripping, stop and jerk techniques, and the like. It is important, when fishing nymphs, to control your line slack. The line should be kept as tight as possible without giving the nymph unintended action. This helps in detecting strikes and in quick hook sets.

## DETECTING STRIKES

With nymphs, strikes tend to be extremely subtle, nothing more than a twitch of the line, an unexpected stop in the current, or a dull feeling to the line. For that reason, many nymph fishermen use strike indicators—tiny floats or pieces of high-visibility thread—to help detect strikes. Another favored approach is to fish a dry fly and a nymph in tandem, letting the high-riding dry fly do double duty as a strike indicator. The disadvantage of this approach is that it can be a difficult rig for the uninitiated to cast without repeated tangles.

# essentials: clothing

Vests come in designs that reach your waist (for most situations) as well as "shorties" or "cut-off" form (for wading and float tubes). Some vests are waterproof—a plus.

Fly-fishing accessories fall into three categories—essentials, those that are useful but not a mandatory part of your equipment, and those which are in effect luxuries. The problem is that where any given item belongs in this categorization depends in part on individual tastes and also on the type of fishing being done. Obviously, for example, a creel has no use for someone who practices nothing but catch-and-release, but it is highly useful for someone who goes on a trip with "release to grease" in mind.

The wisest approach, from the outset, is to examine your situation; acquire the bare necessities; and then add more luxury items as time, need, and your interests dictate.

Waders aside (see pp. 32–33), choose clothing that is comfortable, suitable for the conditions, and in earth-tone colors. You may see bright pastels adorning catalog covers, but you will be better served by drab colors (if you hunt, some of your camouflage attire is ideal).

Generally speaking, it is likely that you already own some clothing suitable for fly-fishing excursions and can easily source the rest—without spending a fortune.

A hat should protect you from sun and rain. Choose a model that fits snugly, or has a chin strap, or some means whereby you can attach it to your vest, so that it does not blow away.

## CLOTHING—THE BASICS

**1 vest**
Most fly-fishing situations dictate wearing a vest, some type of container that fits around your waist or chest, or other means of carrying your gear. Choose a well-made model: most fly fishers cram 10 to 20 pounds of gear into a vest, so tough cloth and sound stitching are in order. Numerous pockets are a plus, though size and convenience rate higher than quantity. Every pocket should close with a zipper or Velcro. D-rings, for attaching accessories such as clippers and hemostats, and a capacious pocket in the back, to store a lunch or rain jacket, are good features.

**2 footwear**
Good footwear, especially if you plan to wade, is essential. Some waders come with boots built in, but you will be better served by buying "stocking-foot" waders and acquiring boots separately. For fishing in rocky streams or slippery conditions, footwear should have felt soles, cleats, tiny suction-cup-like nipples, or some other device to help you keep solid purchase.

**3 headgear**
If you plan to fish in windy conditions, choose a hat with a "stampeded string" or a loop that attaches to the back of your shirt or vest, which may save you from the sad scenario of seeing it floating downstream. A "flat hat" (actually a cap) or a broad-brimmed hat provides protection that shields your eyes, head, and neck from the sun.

# essentials: wading

There are three basic types of wading: wading wet, using hip waders, or donning chest waders. Conditions determine the most suitable approach. In hot weather where water temperatures are in the 60s (16–20°C) or above and with air temperatures in the 80s (26–36°C) or 90s (32–38°C), wading wet adds to your comfort. This can hold true anywhere from a mountain trout stream to working saltwater flats for bonefish. However, in the cool waters trout and salmon require, you don't want to get wet beyond the mid-thigh level. When the weather and/or water dictate the use of waders, hippers are ideal for small streams. Bigger, deeper water demands chest waders.

There are two basic types of both hip and chest waders—stocking-foot waders and those with built-in boots. Stocking-foot models are preferable most of the time. They are more comfortable, less prone to leak, easier to repair when they do leak, more stable (because you are wearing separate boots that usually give more arch support), and lighter in weight. Stocking-foot waders fold up neatly, whereas those with built-in boots are quite bulky to store. Of course, you have to buy separate wading boots with stocking-foot models, but they are well worth it.

### wading boots

Wading boots need to provide traction, comfort, and support. Felt soles or cleats, or sometimes a combination of the two, usually provide the traction. Comfort comes from a good fit and weight. Solid support in the arch and ankle areas is of particular importance, and you may want to give consideration to other factors, such as reinforced toes and the method used to fasten or tie the boots.

Both felt bottoms and cleats will wear out long before the uppers on a good pair of boots, and replacement kits (these are readily available) will extend the life of your footwear. For casual wet wading in still water or on small, shallow streams, you can actually create your own wading shoes

A good wading boot provides plenty of support and a high cut offers protection from bumps and bruises to the ankles. The sole should have studs to provide grip on the slipperiest of surfaces.

from old sneakers, cutouts from outdoor carpeting, and heavy-duty, waterproof glue.

## other wading equipment

Many waders use a wading staff for extra support. Even for the agile, adept wader, a staff can be helpful in fast, powerful water. A wide variety of wading staffs, including collapsible ones, are available. However, you can make a perfectly serviceable one with an old rake or hoe handle, a ski pole, or just a good stout stick.

Gravel guards come in quite handy with stocking-foot waders. These snug tightly around the top of your boots to keep out small rocks and grit. Some stocking-foot waders come with built-in gravel guards.

When wading really big streams, or in the ocean, or when float tubing, you should wear some type of emergency flotation device. Losing your balance in a powerful current or stepping off into a spot over your head can be dangerous. Some fishing vests come equipped with carbon dioxide ($CO_2$) cartridges that can be activated in an emergency, while chest waders often have an inflatable band around the top for emergency use. Most have some means of keeping them tight to your body so they don't fill with water should you take a tumble.

Finally, in dangerous waters it is a good idea to fish with a partner.

Waders need to be breathable as well as waterproof so check the fabric mix. Extra padding around the knees is a good feature to cushion falls. Some chest waders convert to waist models, which can be a bonus.

# other useful equipment

Once you have clothing and footwear needs taken care of, it is time to turn to other necessities.

### fly boxes ▶▶

A sudden gust of wind or slip of the hand can find flies vanishing. Fly boxes don't need to be expensive, and you can use other containers as substitutes. For example, a film canister will hold up to a dozen smaller flies. It is better, however, to have a flip-open box with some means of holding each fly in place.

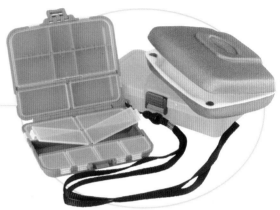

### ◀◀ priest

Essential if you are not catching and releasing, a priest is a wooden (or sometimes metal) baton designed to despatch fish quickly and humanely with a single blow to the top of the head. Check that the implement feels balanced in your hand.

### polarized glasses ▶▶

Polarized sunglasses should always be worn, because they allow you to see through the water. If you don't wear glasses or use contact lenses, a pair of polarized sunglasses will work fine. If you wear glasses to enhance your vision, get polarized prescription eyeglasses or clip-ons.

# hook hone ▸▸

Sharp hooks mean fewer missed fish, and a touch or two from a hook hone, a file made for the purpose, can make a real difference. With most hooks you can determine their degree of sharpness by pulling the point across a fingernail. If they dig in, they are sharp enough.

# ◂◂clippers & zinger

A sportsman without a knife is a lost soul, and a fisherman without clippers might as well be naked. You can buy angling clippers but those you use to trim your nails work perfectly well. A zinger is a clip to hold your accessories, with a retractable cord that attaches to your vest. Choose stainless steel for accessories where possible: it will not corrode.

## FIRST AID KIT

**1** Every fisherman should carry a basic first-aid kit containing:

- bandages
- alcohol wipes
- antibiotic ointment
- aspirin or another painkiller
- waterproof matches
- sun screen
- insect repellent
- scissors
- any prescription medications needed.

## SURVIVAL KIT

**2** Regardless of the conditions at the start of your trip, when in remote country or on backpacking trips, expand your first-aid kit into a survival kit and include:

- a compass
- emergency blanket
- emergency food ration
- heat pack
- cool pack.

If you are going to be really off the beaten track, it is a good idea if at least one of your party has completed an outdoor pursuits first-aid course.

# other useful equipment continued

## ◀◀ waterproofs

Finally, when it comes to "must have" items, don't forget personal comfort and safety. In adverse conditions, you need foul-weather gear, and that means not only waders but also a rain jacket. Getting a soaking, even in a sudden summer thunderstorm, can make you miserable. In cold weather, you can face the threat of hypothermia.

## USEFUL BUT NON-ESSENTIAL ITEMS

**1 CREELS**
These are a must if you keep fish, a non-factor if you don't. Basket or wicker creels have the appeal of tradition, and they can serve as a useful lunch container if you hike into remote areas. Another option is an "Arctic" type creel that keeps fish cool by periodic soakings and through the cooling effect of evaporation.

**4 CAMERA AND FILM**
In today's world of disposable cameras, you can make a lasting record of special moments without adding much weight or danger of destroying expensive camera gear. An inexpensive but perfectly sound way to protect a camera (even a small 35 mm point-and-shoot), along with other items that shouldn't get wet, is a heavy-duty Zip-Lock bag.

**2 VISUAL AIDS**
Getting a tippet through the eye of a size 16 fly in low-light conditions can be a problem, especially as you get older. An inexpensive pair of magnifying glasses of the sort available in most variety stores can be useful. Likewise, a small pen light can be handy if you fish at night.

**5 FISHING DIARY**
This is not something you are likely to carry with you, but it is a good idea to keep a diary (you can, if you wish, do this on computer). A part of the diary might also be a gear list you can check to make sure you aren't leaving something behind.

**3 STREAMSIDE FLY-TYING KITS**
These are useful if you love tying flies or meet a situation where there's a hatch you need to match, but rather bothersome for most.

**6 TAPE MEASURE**
It is necessary if there is a size limit on fish and you intend to keep them. Often these are included on net handles or the top of creels.

## ◀ landing net

A landing net can be cumbersome, but facilitates landing fish. Also, it is much easier to release netted fish unharmed than to handle them excessively. Nets come in many forms—collapsible ones, big ones with long handles for use in boats, slender release nets, those that attach to the back of your vest with a magnet, and more. Frames are usually made of aluminum (which is stronger) or laminated wood.

## rod case ▶▶

Protection for rods (cloth sleeves along with aluminum or plastic tubes) and reels (cases or covers) is important, and the traveling fly fisherman (at least on airlines) will want to acquire a rod case. Zippered outer pockets are a good additional feature, enabling you to carry accessories too. Opt for a lightweight case—you may have to carry it farther than you think.

# luxury items

If you are a gadget freak, there are enough accessories to keep you permanently happy. There's no way we can cover all of them, but a capsule coverage of some should suffice.

## hemostats ▸▸

Although useful for removing flies from fish with sharp teeth, such as big brown trout or, especially, pike, in most situations you don't really have to have hemostats.

## ◂◂ knot-tying tools

Some beginning anglers, along with anyone whose vision is not as acute as it once was, have trouble tying the essential knots. If so, there are devices that will do it for you, saving both time and frustration.

## thermometer ▸▸

A thermometer lets you know the water temperature, and that can be indicative of spawning periods and feeding times, which might help you to locate and catch fish.

## ◂◂ fly drier

Fly, line, and leader treatments include floatants for flies, sinking solutions, leader straighteners, line cleaners, and the like. Use them if you wish, but you can wash a fly off and then blow it dry (or change flies). Use soap and warm water to clean a line, and pulling your leader through a piece of leather or a patch cut from a rubber inner tube will straighten it well.

## THE BARE ESSENTIALS

Some of the items on these pages will undoubtedly be useful, but here is a definitive list of the only items you really need to get out there fly fishing.

| | | | |
|---|---|---|---|
| **1** | Rod and reel | **7** | Vest (with all the key items it should hold—flies, first-aid kit, split shot, nail clippers, hook hone, and the other items you regularly keep in it. Once you have your vest properly equipped, you can store it with the items in place.) |
| **2** | Leaders and tippet material | | |
| **3** | Waders and wading boots | **8** | Net |
| **4** | Shirt and pants | **9** | Waterproof matches |
| **5** | Polarized sunglasses | **10** | Hat or cap |
| **6** | Fishing license | **11** | Rain gear |

Always put your own comfort and safety first. Pack the minimum you need for a good day, but don't sacrifice safety for a couple of extra pounds of weight.

# mastering the basics

Most fly-fishing books for beginners start the "how to do it" aspect of their coverage with information on casting. For all the undeniable importance of casting, however, it is necessary to have your rod fully assembled, with the reel mounted, line strung through the guides, leader tied to the line, and fly attached to the leader's tippet, before you can actually cast to fish. Accordingly, it makes sense to begin with the key knots that enable you to reach the point where you are ready to cast to fish.

# knots sense

The ability to tie a few essential knots must be mastered by every fly fisherman. Knots are nothing more than connectors, and each of the knots described below has a specific function. Those functions include attaching line or backing to a reel, connecting backing or a leader butt to line, joining sections of monofilament, and tying on a fly. There are scores, perhaps hundreds, of knots suited to one function or another, but don't be dismayed. You only need to learn a few of them, at least at the outset. Once you have intimate familiarity with one (or, at most, two) knots for each function, you are suitably prepared for this aspect of the joys of fly fishing.

## ATTACHING LINE TO YOUR REEL

The best knot for attaching line or backing to the arbor on a reel's spool is the Duncan loop (also known as the uni-knot). A weak knot that ties the line to itself, the Duncan loop slides under pressure and thereby allows you to snug the line down on the reel spool.

**1** To tie a Duncan loop, pass the end of the line or backing around the spool and bring the tag back out for 10 inches (25cm) or so. Holding the tag end, turn it back toward the spool to create a loop between the two strands of line.

**2** Then take the tag end and make five wraps around both strands of the line, passing the tag end through the loop as you complete each wrap. Finally, pull steadily on the tag to bring the wraps together.

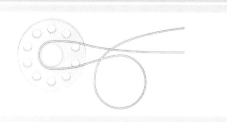

**3** When you wish to replace a line or backing, simply cut the knot loose (you only lose a few inches of line).

## CONNECTING LINE AND LEADER

Linking line to monofilament can pose a problem because of differences in flexibility and diameter. The knot most commonly used to connect line with leader is the tube knot (also known as a nailless nail knot). Instead of the traditional nail, use a 2-inch (5cm) section of a hollow tube (a piece from a soda straw is ideal).

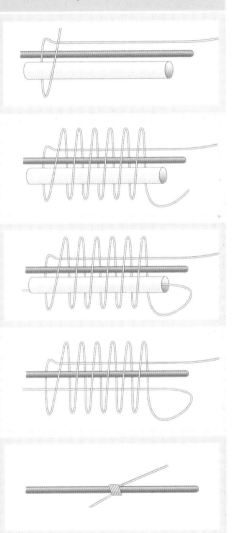

**1** Place the fly line against it with the tag end to the right. Then place the butt section of the leader alongside the tube with its tag end to the left. Make sure you have 12 to 15 inches (30–40cm) of leader left for use in forming the knot.

**2** Hold both line and leader against the tube with one hand while wrapping the leader's tag end around the tube, fly line, and itself (you are reversing directions, left to right). Snug each wrap tightly against the previous one. Use your fingers to keep the wraps tight.

**3** After six wraps, push the leader's tag end back through the tube. Use your left hand to pull the tag end through the tube and slide the tube to the open end (left).

**4** At the same time, pull on the leader's end while maintaining pressure on the wraps. Slide the wraps down close to the end of the fly line. Pull firmly on the tag end and main part of the leader simultaneously to complete the seating process.

**5** Trim the knot closely with clippers and coat it with a light layer of rubber cement so it will flow easily through the rod guides. You only use this knot when you change line or start over with a new leader.

# leader knots

The two knots commonly used to connect one piece of monofilament with another (for constructing a knotted leader or tying a tippet to a knotless leader) are the blood knot and the surgeon's knot. Each has distinct advantages and disadvantages, and both should be learned.

## BLOOD KNOT

The blood knot is the most widely used means for uniting two strands of leader material or tying on a tippet. It works most successfully when the two pieces to be tied are of similar diameter.

**1** Lay two pieces of leader material across each other to form an "X," with 3 or 4 inches (7.5–10cm) of overage with each tag. Wrap one piece of monofilament around the other at least three times, then pull the tag back through the position where the leader pieces originally crossed and hold it in place there.

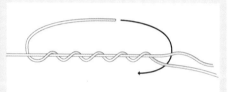

**2** Next, wrap the other piece of leader around the opposite strand the same number of times, making sure you wrap in the opposite direction from that used for the first tag. Bring that tag end back trough the original opening where the two pieces crossed.

**3** Moisten with saliva and tighten the knot by pulling gently on each of the tags until completely firm.

**4** Then clip off as close as possible. This works well in most situations, but a blood knot should not be used when you are dealing with two strands of dramatically different diameters.

## SURGEON'S KNOT

The surgeon's knot is one of the easiest knots to learn and tie, and it can be used to tie pieces of monofilament with varying diameters as well as when using braided-wire material of the sort used in saltwater fly fishing. It is basically an overhand knot that uses both strands of leader at once.

**1** The surgeon's knot is based on the ordinary reef knot, and is bulkier than a blood knot, and more wasteful of leader material. Lay the two pieces to be joined side by side.

**2** Pass the two strands of monofilament through themselves, right over left as you look at the knot. It is easier to work in this way, as if you were starting to tie a bow.

**3** Then pass the strands through the same loop again. (If you want even greater strength, the material could be passed through the loop three times).

**4** After passing the monofilament through the overhand knot's loop, pull the pieces of monofilament simultaneously to tighten. The easiest way to tighten is to pull on both ends. This makes the upper part of the knot twist slightly.

# knots for attaching flies

The knot selected to tie the fly to the leader is obviously crucial—it's the angler's last link. When things go wrong, the knot is often the culprit. Or, more precisely, poor tying of the knot causes the problem. The knot attaching the fly will be the one you tie most often, and familiarity with one of the two knots described below will go a long way toward making you a more effective fly fisherman.

Both the turle knot and the improved clinch knot are standards for tying on flies. Many people prefer the turle knot, primarily because it always aligns perfectly with the fly.

## TURLE KNOT

The turle knot is almost always used for flies for salmon and trout. To tie it, pull the fly onto the tippet, making sure when you do so that the tag end enters the hook eye in the direction of the hook's point.

**1** Slide the hook 12 inches (30cm) or more up the tippet, temporarily out of the way. Then form a loop below the fly by tying a double overhand knot on the tippet.

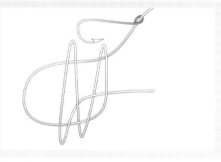

**2** Bring the fly down to the loop, slip the fly through it, and tighten the loop around (not on) the hook eye. When tightening, make sure not to catch any hackle in it. It is imperative that the tippet's tag end remain above the loop.

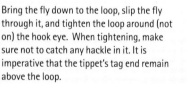

**3** Once you have trimmed the tag, you are ready to start fishing.

There are other knots of potential use in special situations. They include the Bimini twist (used in saltwater fishing) and the Huffnagle knot (for uniting light monofilament to heavy material). In time you may want to learn more, but the knots described here will get you started in fly fishing.

## IMPROVED CLINCH KNOT

Almost everyone who has done any fishing with standard spin-casting or bait-casting gear will already be familiar with the improved clinch knot, because it is commonly used to tie on lures in those types of fishing. Indeed, the knot is so common that many call it the "fisherman's knot."

**1** To tie it, insert a few inches of the leader's tag end through the hook eye, then make at least five turns around the leader above the fly with the tag.

**2** Next, push the tag through the loop you have formed. This forms a simple clinch knot. To complete the improved clinch knot, take one more step—when the tag end passes through the loop, it forms a second loop.

**3** Pass the tag through this second loop, lubricate the knot with saliva, and tighten.

The improved clinch knot, while well known, has several drawbacks. It is difficult to tie with monofilament over 10 lb.-test because of stiffness and the bulk created by the repeated wraps. Also, when using very light tippet in the 1 lb.–2 lb. class range, the knot will occasionally slip or pull out. Finally, this knot can slip around the eye of the hook, which means the fly can land at awkward angles, as opposed to the perfect alignment provided by the turle knot.

# commonsense casting

An aura of mystique seems to surround the art of fly casting. Would-be newcomers are convinced that one of two substantial barriers stand between them and proficiency in wielding a fly rod. Either they believe it is a tedious, time-consuming process filled with frustration or they feel that competent casting requires so much grace and sense of timing few save world-class athletes can master it. These are gross misperceptions.

With a few hours of "hands- on" instruction and a reasonable amount of practice, there's no reason that the beginner should not be able to make casts of 30 to 40 feet (9–12m) with accuracy and delicacy. That is an adequate distance for catching most species of fish. Once you establish the sense of timing and performance good casting requires, considerations such as adding distance, making special casts, and adjusting to special situations can provide challenges to last a lifetime.

For present purposes, though, there is only one critical consideration to keep firmly in mind. It is timing, not strength, which produces smooth casts. Beginners have a decided tendency to try and force the action. In a smooth cast, the rod, not the angler, does the work. However, the caster does control distance, line speed, motion, and timing through the way he handles the rod.

## casting

There are only four basic casts you need to work on at the outset. These are the standard or overhead cast, the backhand cast, the roll cast, and the side cast. Others will come with time if you get the "big four" down pat first.

The four basic casts have similar elements. Line weight makes all of them possible, and preparation for

## GETTING THE ROD READY

**1** Begin by seating the reel with the handle on the side from which you prefer to reel. Next, join the rod pieces, beginning at the butt section and progressing to the tip. It is best to do this by inserting each section's guides at a 90° angle to the previous section. After it is tight, twist as if there were screw threads to align the guides. Reverse the process when taking down the rod. Be sure you know your rod—some ferrules are designed to "marry" without the join seeming to be complete, and too much pressure can throw them out.

**2** When stringing the rod, start by making sure the line leaves the reel at the right place. Pull out a sufficient amount of line to put you 24 inches (60cm) or so past the point where the leader meets the line. Double the line back on itself and push the doubled line through the guides. This way, if the line slips, it will catch at the guide and avoid your having to start over. Also, you are much less likely to miss a guide when you do things this way.

**3** Once you have slipped the doubled line through all the guides, straighten it and the leader out, add a fly, and you are ready to fish. For practice casting, substitute a bit of yarn or use a fly with the hook cut away where it begins to bend.

performing them begins with the angler grasping the rod's handle. The grip should be taken as if you are shaking someone's hand, and the angler's thumb should extend forward pointing toward the rod's tip. You may see other methods of holding the rod, but your thumb is your strongest digit and the one that will make the casting motion easiest. Also, keep firmly in mind the fact that foot position is important. You do not stand with your feet side-by-side as you face your target. Instead, for the overhead cast you "lead" with your "off" foot (your left foot if you are a right-handed caster) and open your shoulders in the direction you wish the cast to travel. This gives you the potential for additional shoulder and hip rotation.

With the rod in your casting hand, use your "off" hand to pull 20 feet (6m) or so of line from the reel. Once you've learned to cast, you will do this in rapid-fire fashion while false casting, but you initially may find this more difficult. When you have some line out, begin moving the rod in a casting motion. The motion "loads the rod" through the weight of the line; this causes the tip of the rod to bend, and as the bend straightens out it sends (in other words, casts) the line through the air.

In the standard forehand cast, the rod bends twice in the course of a single casting cycle—once on the backcast and a second time on the forward cast. In the process, the rod acts as both a spring and a lever.

Prior to casting, you need to get everything ready. Mount the reel on the reel seat, put the rod sections together, string the rod, and tie on a fly.

To cast effectively, grasp the rod as if you were shaking someone's hand, but align your thumb along the rod toward its tip.

# forehand cast

The forehand, or overhead, cast is the one you will use most frequently. In wide open situations, it may well be the only cast you use. The motion will involve the same stroke and rhythm you use for backhand and sidearm casts. Moving and timing are the elements you should seek to master, always remembering to let the rod do the work.

1 Think of the rod as the hour hand on a clock, with your body at 12 o'clock. You should range between 11 o'clock on the forward motion and 1 o'clock on the backward movement. (If you go beyond 10 o'clock or 2 o'clock, you will get yourself into trouble.)

2 Use your free hand to hold the line.

3 Once the rod is loaded, the movement of the rod controls everything. Keep timing in mind—both the timing of rod movement through the casting arc and the pauses between loading the rod at the front and back ends of the arc.

4 Avoid moving forward or back before the line has straightened out and loaded the rod: the whole cast will break down..

5 The timing of the pauses at each end of the casting motion determines the shape of the loop made by the line as it moves through the air. A tight loop means less air resistance and less likelihood of the cast "falling apart." The loop should be a compressed "U" with the legs of the "U" changing their length as the line moves through the air.

6 Keeping your feet still, turn your head to watch cast and backcast to check the tightness of the loop.

## TIP: WATCH THE TIP!

The tip of the rod is the focal point of casting. When you start or stop the rod's tip, you begin to create the loop. The line reacts to the motion of the tip. In that regard, you can get a good idea of your casting motion by tying a bright piece of knitting thread to the tip of a two-piece rod and using this tiny outfit to analyze the elements of the cast and how you perform them.

# backhand, side, and roll casts

## BACKHAND CAST

The backhand cast is nothing more than a forehand cast performed across your body—the casting arm extends across your chest rather than to the side.

**1** Use of the wrist takes on additional significance in the backhand cast, thanks to the fact that you have a more limited range of motion than when using a forehand cast.

**2** You cannot get as much distance with a backhand cast; but in tight conditions, such as when wading an overgrown stream, ability to cast in this manner can be critical.

**3** If you can learn to cast with either hand (in effect, become an ambidextrous caster), you will not need to master the backhand cast.

## ROLL CAST

Frequently you find yourself in positions where any type of backcast is out of the question. For example, when there is a high bank, trees, or bluff behind you; when fishing in strong winds; or when false casts might spook feeding fish. In such situations, a roll cast is the answer, as it is when casting heavily weighted flies. Once you have hit yourself in the head a couple of times casting such flies, you will readily switch to a roll cast.

**1** Roll casting must be done with some line in the water. The surface tension caused by the line being in contact with the water helps load the rod. Raise the tip of the rod slowly to a vertical (12 o'clock) position. It is imperative that the pickup is slow; otherwise, you will jerk the line from the water and lose the needed tension.

**2** When the tip is poised at 12 o'clock, power it forward with far greater impetus than you would employ in an ordinary cast. Then stop the rod tip as you would in a normal cast, with the tip pointing in the intended direction of line flow and with the stop coming close to horizontal (9 o'clock). The line will literally "roll" out in an unfolding "U" curve. If the curve collapses, you probably powered the rod tip too far forward.

**3** The roll cast is fairly easy to learn, although getting much distance can be difficult. A longer rod, which provides some additional mechanical advantage as a longer lever, helps in that regard.

## SIDE CAST

The fourth and final basic cast is the side cast. It actually has two forms—forehand and backhand. Both involve repositioning the rod, as well as the entire casting motion, by 90°.

**1** In other words, you work the rod and line parallel to the water's surface rather than perpendicular to it.

**2** Side casting often comes into play when you fish streams with tree limbs overhead, and it is also an ideal way to get a fly under a dock, beneath streamside or lakeside vegetation, or in any situation where even the tightest of overhead loops would encounter some obstacle.

**3** All elements of the side cast are performed just like the overhead cast—they just take place at a different angle.

## DEVELOPING TECHNIQUE

**1** There are endless theories on the "proper" casting form, but it really is more important to think about the end results than worry about a "locked wrist," "loose wrist," "power shoulder," or the like.

**2** The final judgment on your casting technique can be answered by asking yourself a simple question: "Does it work?" If it does, you will be able to put a fly where you want it with suitable delicacy and efficiency of motion.

**3** Practice is the real key to developing a sound, functional cast. This can be done in your backyard, an open field, or on a pond or stream. Always remember that casting is the means to a desired end—catching fish.

**4** Don't fall into the trap of becoming so immersed in the motions and mechanics (or technique) of casting that you overlook that ultimate purpose.

**5** Most of all, be constantly aware of the fact that casting should be a simple process involving minimal physical effort.

# playing and netting fish

In *The Compleat Angler*, Isaak Walton reminds us that the term fishermen use when failing to land a hooked fish—"losing a fish"—is not exactly accurate. In his words, "A man cannot lose what he never had." That's certainly true, but temporary meaningful connections that end prematurely certainly leave a sense of loss.

Some fish get away no matter how skillfully played, and more are exhausted only to escape thanks to poor landing techniques, such as inept handling of a landing net or gaff. In other words, at an early point in the ongoing education fly fishing involves, an angler needs to be able to play a fish properly and know how to close the deal when it is exhausted.

## playing

With most species of fish, the key to minimizing "losses" is keeping a tight line at all times while letting the rod and reel work for you. Fish easily slip the hook when the fisherman fails to keep steady tension. Use the full length of the rod as a "shock absorber" to protect your tippet, and to help you to land the fish before it is so exhausted that catch-and-release starts to become difficult.

**right** A pull on the line lets you know that a fish has taken the fly, and the challenge to land it starts. Playing fish successfully is largely a matter of practice—the more you do it, the more likely you are to land your quarry successfully.

## SUCCESSFUL PLAYING

**1** Keep in mind that using your "off" hand (the one not holding the rod) to handle the line with a hooked fish, unless it is a small one, can result in a broken tippet. You simply cannot adjust to a sudden run the way a properly adjusted drag can. The idea is to maintain steady pressure, let the fish run against the drag as it wishes, all the while gaining line when the fish allows it.

**2** Once the hook is set, the best thing to do is get the fish "on the reel" as soon as possible. That may involve reeling fast with a fish that runs toward you, even as you hold the rod as high as possible or, more likely, making sure that any slack you were holding in your off hand is smoothly "given" to the fish in its initial run until it is all gone and the line is running from the reel.

**3** Once that has been accomplished, always remember to hold the rod tip high—lines get broken when rod tips are lowered, not to mention that a high rod means the fish is working against maximum resistance.

**4** As the fish tires, you will be able to gain line and eventually bring it close. At that point, with most freshwater species, it is time for a net.

# playing and netting fish continued

### netting

Always aim to bring the fish to the net, not the net to the fish. A sudden swipe with the net often spooks a tired but not completely exhausted fish, and its sudden surge at the most inopportune of moments breaks the leader.

The net should obviously be suited to the size of the fish in question, and the issue of whether you plan to keep the fish for eating purposes also enters into play. Some shallow nets that avoid fish becoming entangled in the mesh are designed specifically for catch-and-release angling. They leave the fish readily accessible, so that a pair of hemostats can grasp the hook, give it a quick turn to remove it, and the fish is ready to return to the water.

**1** If possible, don't even handle the fish, although if it shows signs of being unable to swim away it should be cradled and gently moved back and forth in the current (this forces water through its gills and lets it breathe) until it can swim away on its own.

**2** For larger fish that are to be released, especially in saltwater, the best approach is often to clip or cut the leader as close to the fly as possible and leave it in the fish's mouth. It will soon rust away.

**right** Bring the net to the fish, rather than the other way around. Choose a fine-mesh net so that fish do not slip through, or get lodged in, the fibers.

**3** When you plan to keep fish to eat, dispatch them promptly once they have been landed. Trout and salmon fishermen sometimes carry a stick, much like a policeman's "billy," for this purpose. It is known as a "priest" because it delivers the final rites. For large saltwater fish, a gaff is the order of the day.

**4** Once they have been killed, put fish on ice or in a well-ventilated creel. They will keep better that way; and if the weather is warm, it is also a good idea to clean them immediately.

**5** Checking the stomach contents can also provide insight on what the fish has been eating.

You will make some mistakes along the way in playing and landing fish, and no matter how skilled you become there will be those bittersweet moments when the throbbing pressure of a heavy fish on the line suddenly gives way to dull nothingness. At such times, rather than cursing fate and bemoaning your standing with the angling gods, console yourself with the thought that it is better to have had a temporary connection than never to have hooked a fish at all.

# reading the water

One of the most difficult skills to learn in fly fishing involves reading water. The explanation of why this is the case is a simple one: there's no substitute for experience, and that experience can come only through first-hand observation and wisdom accumulated through hours, days, and years on the water.

Reading the water is, when reduced to its essence, knowing of or sensing the location of fish. There are a number of tips that provide guidance in learning how to read water, but you should always keep in mind the fact that this skill primarily depends on you putting in time fishing. Of course, the learning curve is a pleasant one.

## FOOD AND FEEDING

Fishes' most consistent, constant habit is the need for food, and a keen knowledge of the dietary preferences and habits of a given species will loom large in successful fly fishing. They let you know what fly pattern to offer, how to present it, and where to present it. Accordingly, recognition of the types of places where fish can find food is the key first step in reading water. Most fish that are readily caught on flies get the majority of their food below the surface, and that sends two clear messages:

**1** No matter how much you enjoy fishing with dry flies, nymphs and streamers should loom large in your angling strategy.

**2** The ability to see "through" the water (polarized glasses are essential for this) figures prominently in reading water, because spotting fish is an integral part of the overall "reading" process.

- For the beginner, other, more experienced anglers can help you develop some of the essential "reading" skills. Having a guide or mentor accompany you on the water, pointing out likely holding spots, making observations about fish behavior, and sharing other knowledge can be a big help.

- You can also learn a great deal by maintaining a fishing diary. Whether this is done in a book, on a computer, or simply through handwritten notes, regularly consulting such documentation can be revealing. We will look at specific species in more detail on pages 74–87, but many of the elements of reading water are universal.

As creatures of habit, fish are predictable in many ways and a little knowledge of their habits can reap rewards in terms of locating them.

## SPAWNING BEHAVIOR

Another universal habit is the urge to reproduce. Learning about spawning behavior, favored spawning spots, pre- and post-spawn feeding tendencies, and the like will help. It is also worth noting that several species of fish, including bream, bass, and crappie, are easiest to catch during the spawning period.

## HABITATS

Favored spawning areas constitute one part of a much bigger picture focusing on habitat, where fish are likely to be found at different stages in their life cycle, or at different times of the year. Reading water also means learning to recognize prime holding water, ambush spots, hideouts, and similar areas. Some of these might be easier to detect in summer, when the water is likely to be lower and clearer than it is in winter.

## VISIBLE COVER

Cover is always important, both for predatory fish and for those using it as a place of refuge. The savvy angler instantly recognizes visible cover in forms such as:

1. undercut banks, where there is likely to be overhanging vegetation to hide fish.

2. weed beds, which will similarly hide fish and provide shade, in addition to sheltering many of the insects on which fish feed.

3. rock cast shadows, which have the effect of keeping the water beneath them cool and dark, ideal for surface-shy fish.

4. log jams, which also keep water cool and in shadow, so fish will settle beneath them.

5. jetties, piers, and docks, which all keep water cool and shady, and are liked by many species; food may also accumulate here.

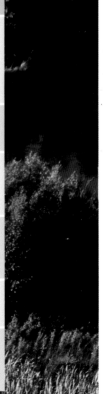

# reading the water continued

## types of water

Fish also choose a particular type of water for reasons of energy efficiency. In currents, for example, they love eddies or places where the stream "breaks its back" on boulders or other structures. Once you learn to recognize spots favored by fish, you have made giant strides in reading the water.

A couple of examples will explain why. Salmon, during their spawning migrations, return to the same pools year after year. Catch one big bass from a particular holding spot and chances are excellent that another fish will take over the location within days. The brown trout fisherman soon learns that the species is supremely energy efficient, hanging out where there isn't much current to fight, and that it also likes dark places such as shaded pools or backwaters close to the main current.

Once you have a pretty sound grasp of habitat, you know preferred places for your cast. Of course, it is still necessary to place the fly in these spots in a realistic fashion. That means reading the water from a different

### SMALL SHALLOW STREAMS

Food will be funnelled to and accumulate in the narrowest areas of a small stream, so look for potential strikes here.

### HOLDING POOLS

Fish are energy efficient and do not spend time fighting the current. Any area behind a rock or other structure, where water is fairly still, will hold fish.

perspective. You need to know the type of cast that will serve you best. With dry flies, for example, avoiding unnatural drag is imperative. The fly needs to be placed where it will be in the fish's window of vision, and whether on the surface or beneath it the action needs to be natural. For example, retrieval speed for a minnow-imitating streamer would be quite different from that for a pattern imitating a lizard or a leech. As a general rule of thumb, make your first cast to the place you think most likely to hold fish. If the situation is one where getting the fly in the right place can be difficult, use simple casts first before "going for broke" with a cast that has a great likelihood of hanging up or going awry in some other way.

Knowing and understanding water, whether it is a fast-flowing mountain trout stream, a slow-moving river, the still waters of a pond or lake, or the vagaries of the ocean, is a subtle skill one never fully masters. You should strive to learn something new every time you fish. There will always be new waters to read and new things to learn in old, familiar waters. In fly fishing in general, and in reading water in particular, there is no graduation day.

## LAKES AND STILLWATER

Where there is no light, there is neither vegetation nor insects on which fish can feed, so the deeper areas of a lake will hold few fish.

## FAST STREAMS AND RIVERS

In fast-moving water, look for natural "holding pools" where you will find fish. These may be behind boulders or structures that break the water flow.

# wading and other maneuvers

**right** Keep safety firmly in mind when wading, particularly if you are alone. It is a good idea to use a staff for extra support. Waders should have felt soles or metal cleats, or both, to give you some purchase on slippery rocks.

No matter how well you cast, you have to get within range of fish in order to catch them. Methods of doing so are a commonly overlooked aspect of fly fishing. Whether you are wading, easing along a bank, gliding through the water in a float tube, or maneuvering into prime position in a drift boat, stealth and savvy connected with getting into position are an important aspect of catching fish.

Experience plays a key role in good positioning, but so do equipment and common sense. This is especially true when it comes to wading, and a lot of fly fishermen fail to approach this aspect of the sport with the same attention they devote to other considerations.

## SAFE AND SUCCESSFUL WADING

There are safety considerations to keep in mind when wading. In rough, deep, or fast-moving water, you should not attempt to cast and wade simultaneously.

Prior to casting get into a suitable position. Plant both feet comfortably, so you face your intended target, and then begin working out line. Sometimes a boulder or other object will diminish water pressure and perhaps help mask your approach as well.

When wading in moving water, "read" the stream for potential wading lanes the same way you would read the water for fish. Often you can reach (and fish) an area of a stream few others fish by switching sides to take the road less traveled.

Using a little ingenuity in wading can pay handsome dividends. Along heavily fished streams, for example, take approaches the average angler would not try. This may mean using streamside vegetation to hide your approach, stalking in a creeping position, or "stooping to conquer" (the knees should be the first part of waders to wear out).

Your wading technique is extremely important. More fish are spooked by inept, awkward, or noisy wading than by sloppy casts. When fishing long, still pools in streams, or glassy-smooth surfaces in saltwater flats, ponds, or lakes, ease through the water with great care. A wake or splash can put fish down in a hurry.

Wading deep can be advantageous. It lowers your profile and puts you closer to being on an "eye level" with fish, although it also makes casting more difficult. Similarly, where the situation exists, try to keep your wading path in shadows as much as possible. The more you blend in with your surroundings, not only in attire but in movement, the better. This is particularly helpful when fishing where there is a lot of angling pressure.

In positioning yourself to cast, keep in mind that fish normally face upstream or into the current. This holds true whether you are in fast-moving trout streams, tidal waters, or even lakes with feeder streams entering them. However, there are occasions where it is better to cast downstream. In crystal-clear creeks or tailwaters, fish may be so spooky the only way to present a fly is for it to drift downstream to them so it is the first thing they see.

Taken in its totality, skillful wading is a distinct advantage and can be quite an equalizer. The angler who is an expert wader can make up for shortcomings in other areas, including casting, and the ability to get into position greatly enhances the likelihood of success.

# fishing while floating

The popular image of the fly fisherman is someone standing knee deep in a stream waving a magic wand, but there are plenty of effective, widely used approaches to the sport that do not involve wading. At least two types of boats—flats boats that are poled and Mackenzie boats—are designed specifically with the fly fisherman in mind. Canoes, miniature inflatable pontoons, and rafts equipped with rowing frames and casting platforms can be used in fly fishing. Then too, there are float tubes (or "belly boats").

Float tubes are ideally suited for ponds, small lakes, or back bays and sloughs in larger lakes. They do have some noteworthy limitations. Float tubes should not be used in moving water; they are unsuitable for fishing far from shore in large bodies of still water; and they have no business sharing the water in places where there are alligators or cottonmouths, or motorboat traffic.

Lightweight and simple to transport when deflated, float tubes can be carried in a backpack to remote

It is almost always quicker and safer to walk to where you intend to fish on shore, then launch your boat or float tube. Most fish will be in less than 20 feet (6m) of water so that crossing the middle of a lake is not necessary.

alpine lakes, and they are perfect for reaching sections of ponds and small lakes you cannot fish from shore or wade. They are also much less expensive than boats. A good float tube will have a comfortable back rest, double chambers, Velcro straps to hold your rod in place when you need both hands free, and some zippered storage pockets. The "seat" area in the middle of the tube should be strong and comfortable, and the entire tube should have some type of tough protective covering. Add a pair of flippers similar to those worn by scuba divers, and you are ready to get down

## SAFETY AFLOAT

**1** Wear a life jacket and hat. There will be glare from the water, so wear polarized sunglasses.

**2** Inflate your tube so that it is firm and almost without wrinkles. A firm tube reduces drag.

**3** Before you get into the water, figure out how you would get to shore if you had a puncture.

**4** Only float in calm water. Watch the approaching weather and do not float in thunder or lightning.

**5** Always carry water, a whistle to attract attention, and a puncture repair kit.

to business by doing a human imitation of a crayfish—all paddling (that is, kicking) sends you backward. It doesn't take long to master a float tube, and the only really difficult aspect of using one is getting into the water.

With belly boats, as with other types of watercraft and when wading, always place primacy on safety, and avoid going out on the water alone. Fly fishing is wonderful fun; but like all water sports, it has an inherent element of danger that should be kept firmly in mind.

A float tube gets you to stretches of water that are impossible to fish from shore, or to wade. Most beginners tend to underinflate their tubes: a properly inflated tube is firm and sits up in the water, making floating faster.

# the joys of tying flies

**below** The rewards of catching a fish on a fly you have tied, and perhaps even designed yourself, are well worth the time and effort involved.

**inset** Your fly does not have to resemble a particular insect. As long as it looks insectlike, it will attract fish.

One of the most widely enjoyed aspects of the sport beyond those cherished hours spent on the water is tying flies. Many anglers find it therapeutic—a welcome escape from the stress and pressures of daily life as well as an exercise in dreaming of fishing trips yet to come. It is also a way of being creative, whether your efforts take you in the direction of framed flies and precision tying or simply an effort to create a new pattern in the never-ending quest to find the perfect fly. Tying flies can also

result in meaningful monetary savings. Big saltwater patterns and salmon flies can cost several dollars each, while you can tie flies for pennies apiece. As long as you don't count the time spent in front of your vise, the potential savings can be significant.

The basic tools of tying are fairly easy to acquire and the requisite skills can be mastered in a short time. There are plenty of kits on the market that will give you all the essentials for getting started, and many fly shops and fishing clubs offer free instruction

(especially during the winter months). Furthermore, there are potential tying materials all around you. If you hunt, everything from deer to wild turkeys, quail to rabbits, offers "stuff" you can turn into fish-catching flies. Of course you can buy an endless variety of material from the same folks who sell tying kits, hooks, and related items. Once they get into it, many fly fishermen find that sessions at the vise offer them a great deal of quiet satisfaction, and certainly there are few more rewarding aspects of the fly-fishing experience than catching fish on flies you have tied.

## TOOLS FOR TYING YOUR OWN FLIES

At the outset, fly tying need not be costly or complicated. With some basic items and the raw materials for tying flies, you can concoct deceitful creations that catch fish. Here's a working list of equipment you should have to get started, beginning with five absolutely essential items.

**1** VISE—The key tool. It should be adjustable in terms of height and should have adjustable jaws that will accommodate hooks of all sizes.

**2** SCISSORS—These should have fine points and keen cutting edges suitable for working with tiny bits of hackle or performing precision cuts.

**3** BOBBIN—Make sure you get one with a long, smooth barrel, and a high quality tension-adjustment apparatus.

**4** HACKLE PLIERS—There are many styles of hackle pliers, but most feature one jaw with rubber coating and one of serrated steel.

**5** BODKIN—Just a sharp-pointed instrument for applying head cement, clearing glue from hook eyes, and similar tasks. A bodkin is also useful for working "wind knots" loose from monofilament. Any sturdy, sharp-pointed item will work.

Vise, scissors, bobbin, and hackle pliers should all be of high-quality steel and should last a lifetime.

There are a lot of other useful gadgets available. High on the list should be a whip finisher (a device that wraps thread more rapidly and tighter than you can with your fingers), a hair stacker to help keep hair and similar material even when you use it for wings on flies, beeswax (or other dubbing wax) to help hold material in place until cement is applied, a bobbin cleaner, a small file, and a half-hitch tool. You will also need a selection of hooks for the type of flies you intend to tie, along with selections of the four major categories of materials—thread, body materials, hackles, and wings and tails. You can purchase almost everything you need, but collecting materials from nature when hunting, for example, is enjoyable and saves money.

# savoring secrets

The creative process as it relates to fly fishing—making items ranging from the functional to a level of fine art—is one popular way of deriving a fuller measure of pleasure from the sport. Such pursuits, though, are not for everyone. When it comes to the process of discovery or creating a storehouse of "secrets," however, everyone bitten by the fly-fishing bug has to be intrigued.

## knowledge gathering

Almost all experienced anglers have what might be described as secrets—remote pools or streams they know about, hidden lakes, off-trail destinations overlooked by others, and the like. There are also secrets of a different kind—especially effective techniques, fly patterns that work wonderfully well in a particular region, or inside knowledge of a spawning run or little-utilized species. In truth, secrets is not really the right word to use, although it seems to be the one fly fishermen favor. What veteran anglers accumulate are tidbits of wisdom, garnered through the school of experience, that collectively make the angler better at catching fish.

Some insight on such matters, if shared with the tyro, may smooth the path you take on your fly-fishing apprenticeship. An excellent place to begin concerns the angler as a predator. As humans, we have always been predators, and stalking fish can

be both challenging and rewarding. The first aspect of stalking is locating fish, often with the use of polarized glasses, careful approaches, and close attention for any signs of feeding activity. Once fish have been located, the next step is figuring out a way to get a fly to the proper place, and, hopefully, draw a strike.

## new challenges

Anglers have a tendency to talk about "impossible fish," but in reality there's no such creature. There are just difficult fish—ones that pose particular problems because of inherent wariness, or where they are located, or for some other reason. Remove the word "impossible" from your fly-fishing vocabulary and view such fish simply as special, and welcome, challenges.

## TIPS FOR MORE CONSISTENT FLY FISHING

You may have to take unorthodox measures: approach a spot from an unlikely angle, crawl to get into position, cast from your knees or while barely peeking over a boulder, or some other tactic. Learning to employ unorthodoxy when needed is one hallmark of an accomplished angler.

Always make sure your hooks are sharp (pulling a fly across your thumbnail to see if it "grabs" is a good way to do this). A sharp hook is easier to "set" in the fish's mouth, and is easier to remove, whether you are catching and releasing or keeping the fish to eat.

Make every effort to fish efficiently. Lots of false casting is unproductive. It tires you out and flies in the air don't catch fish. Practice casting in your yard, so that when you are on the water you cast effectively.

# savoring secrets continued

## TIPS FOR MORE CONSISTENT FLY FISHING

Don't overlook the virtues of patience and persistence. Sometimes you can drift a fly past a feeding or resting fish dozens of times, then suddenly, when nothing seems any different from all the other presentations, you get a bite.

**4**

Avoid the temptation to be a fair-weather fisherman. Adverse weather conditions virtually guarantee less competition from other anglers, and in today's angling world gear is available to enable you to fish in comfort.

**5**

Some fish actually seem to be more active in certain kinds of "bad" weather. Brown trout, for example, are notorious for their preference for low-light conditions, and an overcast day with drizzle can be ideal for them.

**6**

**above** Brown trout prefer low-light conditions.

Salmon often await heavy rains and rising waters before moving into spawning grounds, and rain can be a catalyst for heavy feeding with many species of fish. Showers or heavier rains, especially when accompanied by winds, wash lots of food into the water and can trigger feeding frenzies. When this happens, even the grayest of days can be glorious.

Although it doesn't fall into the category of enhanced skills or improved fishing, don't overlook the vital matter of fishing ethics. Steer clear of other anglers who are already casting in a pool or stretch of water, do your part to ensure the future of the sport, think about sharing angling's joys with youngsters, and, of course, always obey fishing regulations.

Sound ethics, an eagerness to learn, and an ongoing process of discovery will mean that you enjoy each step of the endless journey that is the fly-fishing experience. You will never achieve complete mastery, and you will never learn all the secrets. But that's just as well, because an angling world without the promise of new horizons would be a dreary world indeed.

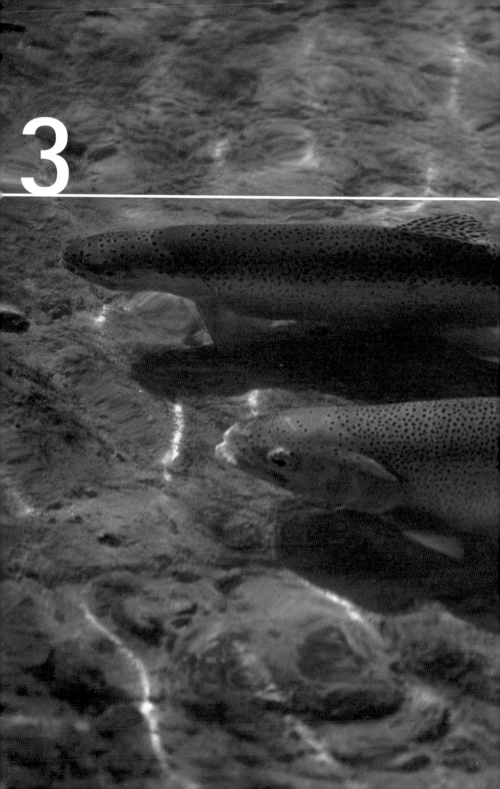

3

# quarries for fly fishing

This chapter looks at the enormous variety of species available to the fly fisherman, wherever he is, and whatever his experience, although the nature of this book means that the most accommodating, most common, and most satisfying in terms of sport and environment are listed first. You will find here information on the fish, their preferred habitats—and therefore places where you are more likely to locate them—the best combinations of rod, line, and flies, and some top tips for successfully striking your preferred quarry.

# panfish: perfect for starting out

Panfish are ideally suited for getting an introduction to fly fishing. Whatever your approach, and whether you fish for bluegills, crappie, or other sunfish, these small, plentiful species are an ideal quarry for the beginning fly fisherman. They provide the chance to get ready for more challenging fish, but even for the expert they remain loads of fun.

For several reasons, there is a staunch argument for the pleasures of panfishing.

- Prolific by nature, panfish are also widespread. In all likelihood, they are found in a pond, stream, or lake close to where you live.
- They are quite cooperative when it comes to hitting a wide variety of fly patterns, because a major portion of their diet is comprised of insects.
- They can be quite forgiving when it comes to sloppy casts.
- For their size, they are capable of putting up a strong fight.
- Properly cooked, they make fine fare.

## EQUIPMENT FOR PANFISHING

| ROD | FLIES |
|---|---|
| Virtually any balanced outfit will work for panfish, although lightweight ones (2-, 3-, or 4-weight) let the fish display their sportiness to the best advantage. If there is a possibility of hooking a bass, which happens quite often, you might want to consider a heavier weight rod. The same holds true in windy conditions or when, for some reason, you need extra casting distance. | **1** Panfish eat a little bit of everything, although crappie, which prefer minnows, are a notable exception to this. |
|  | **2** **In warm weather** There's nothing quite like a small popping bug (hook size 10 or 12), although dry flies of the sort commonly used for trout fishing also work perfectly well. |
| **REEL AND LINE** | **3** **For action beneath the surface** Opt for small nymphs, such as a Hare's Ear or Pheasant Tail, and don't overlook small, slowly worked streamers, such as a Muddler Minnow. |
| With panfish the reel is not a factor. A floating line will suffice, but sink-tip lines are nice when the fish are several feet below the surface. As for leaders, 7 feet (2m) or so is plenty of length, and panfish are seldom leader shy, so a tippet in the 4-lb. test (or more) range is quite satisfactory. | **4** You can also handle tiny jigs ($\frac{1}{16}$ ounce is ideal) with a fly rod, though they are a bit difficult to cast. |

left Panfish are easier to catch post-spawn. Warmer water in spring prompts spawning, so they are abundant in spring and summer. They hug the bank where food is plentiful and are easy to catch from a boat or float tube.

## PANFISHING

### LOCATING PANFISH

**1** Panfish, except for crappie, spend most of their lives near shore or in shallow water. This offers them ready access to the cover that simultaneously provides food and protection.

**2** Because of their habitat preferences, panfish are convenient for the bank fisherman or those who want to wade a pond's edge. Just ease along, covering two or three feet (0.5–1m) of water each time you cast, take a step or two, and repeat the process.

**3** A more versatile approach is to fish from a canoe, john boat, or float tube. Ease along parallel to shore while casting to likely spots. You can also use front and back anchors to stay stationary when that is desirable.

### TOP TIPS

**1** Rig a popping bug or buoyant dry fly in tandem with a nymph and let it do double duty as a strike indicator. This rig is created by tying a piece of monofilament to the bend in the hook and attaching a second fly (the nymph) to it. Cast as you would a single fly, although you will need better form to turn the tandem rig over smoothly. Sometimes you get a double-header, especially with bedding bream.

**2** There are some simple tricks of the panfishing trade worth remembering. For starters, keep in mind the fact that long casts aren't important, but patience is. Often when a fly or popper lands in still water, a bream will approach it immediately but delay striking. Wait until the concentric circles disappear, then give the fly just the slightest of twitches. After two or three such wait-and-twitch approaches, you can "pop" the bug hard if you want, then retrieve and cast again.

# trout, salmon, and steelhead

Trout, salmon, and steelhead are widely reckoned to be the premier fly-fishing species. They enjoy historic appeal connected with the sport's roots, are most often found in beautiful settings, and their habitat needs of cold, clear water add to their appeal. These species thrive in a wide array of habitat, from tiny rivulets and beaver ponds to tailwaters and mighty rivers. Still, they are fragile, demanding unpolluted water, minimal siltation,

## LOCATING TROUT, SALMON, AND STEELHEAD

| PONDS AND SMALL LAKES | SMALL STREAMS |
|---|---|
| **1** In more northern climes, trout do well in smaller bodies of still water provided that these bodies of water have sufficient oxygen and do not freeze solid in the winter. | **1** Small streams offer a lot of advantages for the beginning fly fisherman:<br>■ they do not require long casts to reach most areas<br>■ wading usually presents no major problems<br>■ water in them is much easier to read than in large rivers or still water.<br>In short, streams that are only 30–40 inches (75–100cm) wide (or less) can be appealing. |
| **2** In the West, stock ponds and alpine lakes, along with small spring-fed bodies of water created with fishing specifically in mind, are home to species of trout. | |
| **3** The above holds true for beaver ponds in many colder areas, and brook trout in particular seem to thrive in still water. | **2** The standard approach is to wade upstream, no matter what type of fly is being used. It makes the drift of dry flies and mending line easier, and you are less likely to spook upstream-facing fish. |
| **4** Fishing can present special problems. Trout in such habitat spook easily, and getting within reasonable casting distance without being seen can pose problems. | **3** Small streams seldom hold lunker fish, although in really fertile waters there can be noteworthy exceptions. Still, these streams offer all sorts of special rewards: oneness with your prey, greater likelihood of enjoying the solace of solitude, and the soothing rhythm of gurgling, tumbling water. |
| **5** Float tubes are often the best approach. A float tube makes for stealthy approaches and lets the angler cast to places he cannot reach from shore. | **4** Most trout streams are free flowing, but don't forget that creeks, depending on the nature of the habitat they offer and where they are found, can hold many other species of fish as well. |
| **6** Fly fishing on ponds and small lakes allows you to observe hatches, feeding, and the like. | |

plenty of oxygenation, and water temperatures that never get really warm. For these reasons, they are somewhat limited in geographical range, though in the United States they are generally found as far south as Georgia along the spine of the Appalachian mountains.

These fish, collectively known as salmonids, take flies readily. Add to that factor their sleek, streamlined beauty, spectacular leaping abilities, and sheer power, and their appeal is easily understood. Given their appeal, we will take a detailed look at the species, along with where they are found.

| LARGER RIVERS | TAILWATERS | LARGE LAKES |
|---|---|---|
| **1** Big, brawling rivers pose all sorts of special problems but they are also seasonal homes to salmon and steelhead as well as year-round habitat for trout. This is where you often find larger fish. | **1** Although an unintended benefit, literally hundreds of miles of premier trout water have been created by man as a byproduct of dams built for flood control and power production. The outflows from the lakes thereby created are known as tailwaters, and thanks to being cold, highly oxygenated, and rich in nutrients, they form a fine place to grow big trout. | **1** Big lakes usually present big problems for trout and salmon fly fisherman thanks to the fact that it is difficult to locate fish at depths that are manageable with a fly rod. |
| **2** These rivers are often difficult for beginners. They can demand long casts, far more skill in reading the water, and can be difficult or impossible to wade. | | **2** At times, however, when trout are feeding on the surface or close to shore, the fly fisherman can have his day on such bodies of water. |
| **3** If you do fish such waters when starting out, a guide or fellow angler with local knowledge and experience is recommended. | **2** Most wade fishing in tailwaters is done when the water is "off" (when the dam gates are closed), but they can be fished from boats when it is "on." | **3** In large bodies of water, trout often feed next to trashlines comprised of logs, sticks, leaves, and other flotsam. Also, when it is windy, fish shorelines where the wind is pushing against the shore. This drives surface insects and small baitfish to that shore. That in turn attracts fish. |
| | **3** Most tailwaters have little if any natural reproduction by trout, but stocked fish attain record size in them. | |

# trout, salmon, and steelhead continued

Since trout species vary appreciably in their habitat preferences, feeding patterns, and behavior in general, a brief overview of each of the major ones might be helpful. Of course, it should also be noted that it is common to find two or three species of trout in the same stream or body of water.

## SPECIES OF TROUT

| RAINBOW TROUT | CUTTHROAT TROUT |
|---|---|
| The rainbow trout, with the vivid lateral stripe from which it takes its name, has always been a favorite of fly fishermen. Acrobatic when hooked, and widespread across the country, 'bows are the premier species of fast-flowing freestone streams. | "Cutts" are widespread in the West, and there are several subspecies. All get their name from the bright, distinctive slash that adorns their gill plates. Aside from this characteristic, they resemble rainbows and the two species sometimes cross. |

### FLIES
Rainbow trout take a wide variety of insect patterns readily, and larger rainbows also will hit flies imitating minnows, crayfish, and other larger food items.

### FLIES
Like brook trout, cutts can be quite easy to catch, although where they get a lot of pressure it's another story entirely. They are a wonderful dry-fly quarry, especially in fast-moving streams, but nymphs or a combo dry fly–dropper rig also works well.

### LOCATING RAINBOWS
Rainbows are much less light sensitive than other species of trout and surface feed readily, even in bright sunshine.

### LOCATING CUTTHROATS
Cutts are found up and down the spine of the Rockies, mostly in pristine surroundings with clear, quite cold water. They readily hit a wide variety of flies and are eager surface feeders.

| STEELHEAD | BROOK TROUT |
|---|---|
| Steelhead trout are rainbows that live in saltwater or large freshwater lakes, only entering streams during the spawning season. They also differ from rainbows in color, at least when first entering streams after living in the depths, in that they are bright silver. Steelhead grow quite large and, like salmon, return to spawn in the river where they were born. | Also known as brookies, specks, speckled trout, and natives, this species is really a member of the char family. However, because they are commonly called trout and show the basic habit and habitat characteristics of trout, they are included here. |

## FLIES

Steelhead usually strike out of irritation or reflex, and brightly colored fly patterns fished deep seem to be most productive.

## FLIES

Brook trout, particularly small ones, are the easiest of all trout to catch. They readily hit dry flies and nymphs. Bright flies, such as a Royal Humpy, Royal Wulff, or indeed any attractor pattern, seem to draw ready strikes.

## LOCATING STEELHEAD

A useful approach is to find "stacked" steelhead as they rest during their spawning migration and then to concentrate on these holding pools.

## LOCATING BROOK TROUT

With little tolerance for pollution, siltation, or warm water temperatures, brook trout are normally found where human intrusions have been minimal.

## TOP TIP

Often a sinking line helps, and a willingness to make lots of searching casts and also to cover the water methodically are integral parts of the sport.

## TOP TIP

They like stiller waters, even in fast-moving streams. In moving water, look for them in long, still pools or places where they do not have to fight the current.

# trout, salmon, and steelhead continued

## BROWN TROUT

A European import, browns are the wiliest, wariest member of the trout family. Reclusive by nature, they rarely feed in bright sunlight, preferring low-light conditions and dark hideaways. Dawn and dusk, along with overcast or rainy days, are prime times to catch them.

### FLIES

Small brown trout feed heavily on insects; then, as they grow, they become more nocturnal in their habits and more prone to eat large items. Simply put, big browns like big bites. Usually they require accurate casting and perfect presentation.

### LOCATING BROWNS

Their preferred lies include eddies, undercut banks, backwaters, and about anywhere the stream breaks its back.

## OTHER TROUT

There are a number of other species of trout, mostly confined to a few areas or special habitats. These include:

- lake trout
- Dolly Varden or bull trout (they are actually a char)
- golden trout
- Apache trout, and others.

Bull trout are protected in almost all of the few streams where they are still found in the Lower 48, and there are few places where you can fish for them.

Gold trout have been successfully stocked in a number of alpine-like lakes in the Rockies. Often a rugged hike into remote country can provide excellent fishing for the species some consider the most lovely of all trout.

The Arctic grayling and char are not trout species, but these residents of the far North—Canada and Alaska—do deserve brief mention since they hit flies well, and both are fish of stunning beauty.

## SPECIES OF SALMON

### ATLANTIC SALMON

The single species of salmon to inhabit the Atlantic Ocean reigns in many minds as the king of fly fishing. Their original range has been dramatically reduced, and today most prime Atlantic salmon water requires something close to the key to Fort Knox in order to be able to fish for them.

Unlike the various Pacific salmon, Atlantic salmon survive spawning and may return two or more times to fertilize or lay eggs.

### FLIES

Bright flies cast across the current allowing the line to swing downstream with the fly a few inches under the surface induce the most strikes. The hookset is rather specialized, with most first-timers setting the hook too rapidly. Once hooked, Atlantic salmon are prone to jump numerous times while making powerful runs.

### LANDLOCKED SALMON

Except for being smaller in size, these are similar to Atlantic salmon and have been introduced to the Great Lakes and elsewhere. Other than during spawning runs, they are too deep for fly fishing. Another freshwater, landlocked salmon is the kokanee. They feed primarily on microorganisms and are difficult to catch on a fly.

### PACIFIC SALMON

In contrast to the single species of Atlantic salmon, there are several species of salmon found in the Pacific. These include:

- king (or Chinook)
- silver (or coho)
- humpback (or pink)
- chum (or dog)
- sockeye (or blueback).

They are caught during their spawning runs, and fly fishermen like to deal with them when they first arrive from the sea. At that point, they still have their bright silver coloration (which turns to red as the spawning run progresses) and all their formidable strength. Once they enter freshwater all that really concerns them is spawning, so when strikes occur they are only incidental to movement upstream.

### FLIES

Bites come from irritation or instinct, rather than hunger. Bright streamers are the most effective flies for Pacific salmon.

# the beauties of bass

Most people associate bass with sleek 150-horsepower boats, keenly competitive tournaments, and bait- or spincasting gear. Yet largemouth and smallmouth bass, and to a slightly lesser degree, stripers, are a wonderful quarry for the fly rodder. In fact, during warm weather and in the right situation, a fly fisherman can hold his own and maybe then some when it comes to pure bass-catching effectiveness (and have a wonderful time in the bargain).

## EQUIPMENT FOR BASS FISHING

### ROD

For bass fishing, you will want at least a 7-weight rod. In most conditions, an 8- or 9-weight is even better. That gives you plenty of backbone to cast and for setting the hook with authority. Longer rods are preferable, especially if you are casting from a sitting position in a canoe or float tube.

### TAPER AND LEADER

Outfit the rod with a bug taper (a heavy, short taper intended to push bulky flies through the air), and you won't need a leader longer than 9 feet (3m) at most. It can and should be quite strong—bass aren't particularly leader shy and you'll need strength to "horse" larger bass from weeds or other structures.

### FLIES

**1** Popping bugs are probably the most popular fly-rod offerings for bass. They are big and because of air resistance can be somewhat difficult to cast, but the fact that they land with considerable noise doesn't really matter. In fact, the noise often attracts the attention of bass.

**2** Streamers and larger nymphs also are effective for bass. One of the great advantages of a fly rod for bassing is that it lets the angler reach prime places that are not nearly so accessible to standard gear.

**3** With smallmouth bass, patterns that imitate key items in their diet—hellgrammites, crayfish, dragonflies, and minnows—are good choices, as are the same popping bugs and sliders (another type of topwater offering) largemouth find attractive.

## LOCATING BASS

**1** We tend to associate bass with ponds and lakes, but they are also widely found in streams. As America's most popular game fish (though not with fly rodders), bass are widespread. Largemouth can tolerate a wide variety of water conditions, while smallmouth require cleaner, cooler water. Chances are that no matter where you live there are bass nearby in a farm pond, municipal lake, large reservoir, or stream.

**2** Most portions of larger bodies of still water are in effect "off limits" to the fly fisherman because of depth, but he can own the shorelines and shallow areas. Also, when fish are chasing bait near the surface in deeper portions of a lake, the fly rodder can get in the game.

## STRIPED BASS

Striped bass fishing, whether in saltwater or freshwater, is a bit more specialized. It requires longer casts, and the ability to punch out casts of 70 feet (21m) or more really helps. This means using big rods with reels featuring effective drag systems and holding plenty of backing. Catching bass in still water usually requires watching and waiting for surface action, then getting the fly into feeding frenzies in a hurry. White bass, hybrids, and largemouth also "herd" minnows to the surface at times. Another approach with striped bass is to fish for them in streams when they make their annual spawning runs.

No matter which bass you try with the fly, you are in for considerable excitement. You likely will learn why Dr. James Henshall, the father of modern bass fishing, once stated that "inch for inch, and pound for pond, the black bass is the gamest fish that swims."

## TOP TIPS

**1** When it comes to largemouth bass, spring and fall are the best seasons for the fly fisherman, and in many parts of the country May and September are months of sheer magic.

**2** Shoreline structures of almost any kind—docks, drop-offs, rocks, and logs—are all places worth probing, and at dawn and dusk fish often roam the shallows seeking a meal.

**3** Smallmouth bass are also a great fly-rodding quarry, and when hooked they are spectacular fighters—Tennessee novelist Caroline Gordon once described them as "chicken hawk and chain lightning."

**4** The key word in dealing with bronzebacks, as smallmouth bass are often known, is rocks. They always seem to concentrate around them.

**5** For beginners and veterans alike, the biggest problem in fishing for bass is impatience. An old adage connected with topwater lures suggests "wait until you can't stand it, and then wait that much longer" before imparting action to the popper. After a long period (as much as 30 seconds) of letting the bug sit still, give it a twitch. If that doesn't draw a strike, then it is time to try "popping" it with a sharp jerk or maybe an erratic stop-and-go retrieve. With streamers and other sub-surface flies, of course, you can strip and stop, use a steady retrieve like minnow swimming, or employ other approaches. Experimentation to see what works best is always a good idea.

# other freshwater species

In addition to the species already mentioned, there are scores of other freshwater fish that can be caught while fly fishing and several species that provide wonderful sport for the fly fisherman.

## PIKE AND MUSKIES

Northern pike and muskies present a gratifying challenge to the fly fisherman.

### ROD AND LINE

Because their razor-sharp teeth can sever monofilament with ease, it is normal to use big shock tippets or even some type of wire tippet.

You also want the advantages offered by a big rod (at least an 8-weight), with plenty of backbone and perhaps a fighting butt.

The hookset on these tough-mouthed species needs to be of the "serious business" sort a stiff, strong rod provides.

### FLIES

When northern pike are in shallow water they often hit streamers or big topwater flies with a will.

## CATFISH

Plentiful almost everywhere, catfish are true brawlers when hooked as well as wonderful eating fish.

Channel cats, often found in moving water or in tailraces where turning turbines chop up bait fish, are especially sporty.

You need to get deep for them, because they are a bottom fish, and a sinking line or use of split shot is imperative.

### FLIES

Streamers work best for catfish, and because they feed by smell at least as much as by sight, it isn't a bad idea to "cheat" a bit by using one of the many commercial scents to dress your fly a bit.

**right** Water quality, temperature, and time of year play a part in what you might catch with your fly rod. If you are not choosy, there are plenty of species in rivers and lakes to give you a good day's sport.

## CARP

Another frequently scorned fish that will give any fly rodder about all he can handle is the lowly carp. One of any appreciable size hooked on a fly will battle fiercely.

### FLIES

The key with carp is to find a fly, usually tiny, that imitates the algae and related items of its diet.

One tip in that regard is to do some "vegetarian" chumming. Throw some coarsely ground cornmeal or crumbled fish pellets in the water; then, once the carp find it and start feeding, offer them a sparsely dressed nymph on a small hook that looks like the chum.

If your line moves or twitches at all, set the hook; then get the fish on the reel immediately.

## WHITEFISH

In the Rockies, whitefish are often viewed as trash fish; but any fish that lives in clean water and beautiful surroundings, that will take a fly (dry fly or nymph) readily, and that will give a good account of itself when hooked deserves respect. In fact, whitefish have more than once made what would otherwise have been indifferent days for trout a real delight.

### FLIES

The patterns and presentations that work for trout (see pp. 78–80) are also effective on whitefish. Trout and whitefish often share the same habitat, so when you are fishing for trout, a whitefish may well take your fly.

Keep in mind the fact that whitefish have quite small mouths, so hook size is a factor. Beadhead nymphs tied on size 14 hooks or smaller, along with sparsely dressed dry flies on similar hook sizes, are just the ticket.

# other freshwater species continued

## SHAD

Although it is strictly a seasonal thing focused on their spring runs into coastal rivers, shad can provide fly fishermen with some great action. A hooked shad defines power.

### FLIES
Most shad are caught on sparsely dressed flies tied on Sproat hooks and featuring bright colors. Attractor beads are sometimes added at the end of the tippet, although they make casting somewhat difficult. Fortunately, casting isn't much of a factor, because the standard tactic is to get a fly deep enough in a pool (use of split shot to keep it there is often necessary). It is, in effect, stationary trolling, and patience is imperative. Sooner or later, though, a shad will get irritated enough to strike, and then the fight is on.

## CHUBS

"Chubs" is a generic term fly fishermen use to embrace any of a number of oversized minnows or so-called "trash" fish. Yet the fact that such fish readily hit flies and in many cases give a fine account of themselves for their size makes them worthy of some attention. They also offer an ideal way to introduce a beginner to basic skills such as presentation, mending line, hook setting, and handling fish once they have been hooked.

### FLIES

Fly pattern for chubs seldom makes much difference. Opportunistic feeders (and potential pests when your focus is on something like trout), they feed on whatever happens to be available. If you are just fooling around or practicing, this is a good opportunity to get a final bit of mileage out of frayed flies or ones that have begun to come apart.

## OTHER SPECIES

There are countless other freshwater species that can be caught on a fly.

**1** Bowfin and gar take flies readily, although getting a hook set in their bony mouths can be difficult.

**2** Walleye can be taken on brightly colored streamers, particularly during their spring spawning runs.

**3** Anyone who has spent much time fishing for trout realizes that any number of other fish readily take his flies, and these are generally covered under chubs. However, larger freshwater fish such as fall fish, mooneye, goldeneye, redhorse, herring, and even suckers can be caught on flies. In short, whether your focus is game fish or trash fish, mighty salmon to tiny panfish, the fly rod can provide plenty of freshwater fun.

# the pros and cons of guides

A good guide, particularly at the outset of the fly-fishing experience or when you are fishing new territory, can greatly increase the likelihood of success. Note, however, the emphasis on the word "good." An inept, indifferent, or surly guide means a pricey and unpleasant outing. Much the same holds true for outfitters with whom you might plan to spend several days or a week.

## WILL A GUIDE BE HELPFUL?

There is the question of "guide versus no guide." Even for the experienced angler who is in new waters, there's no question that a capable guide can be helpful.

**1** He will know the best places to fish.

**2** He will know what flies are most productive, and what techniques to use.

**3** If you are budget-conscious, one good idea is to hire a guide for a day with the idea in mind that you will pick his brain about local hotspots.

**4** Observe his techniques closely, and generally seek to garner enough information to go it alone for the rest of your trip.

**5** You might even tell him what you plan and, if you feel you get really sound insight and advice, tip accordingly.

Fortunately, there are steps you can take to determine the quality of the person you are dealing with.

### seeking references

First and foremost, ask for references and follow through on them. Anyone who is reluctant to provide references should immediately become suspect, while those who do provide references should still be checked out thoroughly. Ask previous clients some hard questions such as: "Would you hire this person again?," "Did you catch fish?," "Was the overall experience worth what you paid?," and "Did you learn anything from the guide?" If you get equivocal answers to these and related questions, you should have second thoughts. Also, check out at least three references you are offered. A few dollars spent on phone calls can save you a lot of wasted dollars spent on a bad experience.

### do some research

Another approach is to do plenty of homework in advance. Local visitors' bureaus or chambers of commerce almost always have some literature on fishing, and through the Internet there's a world of information at your fingertips. Acquire some topographical maps, maybe buy a guidebook or two, and, then, when you arrive on location, ask some probing questions at the sporting goods store where you purchase your license or pick up a few last-minute fishing needs. Don't expect to learn about every local hotspot, but you should obtain some sound general information.

## other anglers

Once you go fishing, if you are on your own, take advantage of any opportunities offered by chance encounters with local anglers. A polite conversation can often lead to lots of information or maybe even an invitation to accompany the person you meet to spots he knows about. Such serendipity can be one of the sparkling highlights of any fly-fisherman's experiences, for they sometimes turn just another outing into the trip of a lifetime.

**below** A good guide or outfitter will be interested in you catching fish, and offer instruction and advice to enable you to do so. You can, of course, often get this information for free from fellow anglers.

# reading water—safely!

Although "reading" water receives considerable attention here from the standpoints both of finding fish and maneuvering into place so as to be able to cast to those fish (see pp. 58–61) a few additional pointers are in order.

## FINDING FISH

**1** There are almost always areas of water, especially in streams, that hold few if any fish. By knowing their characteristics, you can avoid wasting a good deal of your precious fishing time probing unproductive waters.

**2** Where there is little, if any, structure you are not going to find many fish.

**3** Structure in whatever form—rocks, logs, undercut banks, weeds or other vegetation, and the like—provides a refuge for smaller fish, and serves as both an ambush spot and a likely source of food for larger ones.

**4** Very shallow water in streams seldom holds fish, except when the light is quite low.

**5** The same holds true for exceptionally fast-running water as well as for long, "dead" stretches where there is very little current.

## SAFETY

**1** In reading water from the standpoint of wading, keep safety firmly in mind. Remember that exceptionally clear water is almost always deeper than it seems.

**2** What seems moderate current strength when you are wading at knee depth can be a powerful one when you are in above your waist.

**3** Always be aware of the dangers posed by slick rocks. Moss and accumulated silt can make rocks extremely slippery.

**4** Round, smooth rocks invariably offer less purchase than ones with an edge. In rugged, remote streams, be especially careful when it is necessary to do some climbing or scrambling to get from one pool to the next.

**5** Basically, use common sense and a good, solid dose of caution in your wading; and if your "read" of a given situation sends up even the slightest bit of a red flag, don't try it.

# fly fishing in saltwater

Saltwater fly fishing is specialized, but it has soared in popularity over the last generation or so.

## flats fishing

Most of the interest focuses on fishing flats for bonefish, tarpon, permit, and other species found in flats. Fishing is done by sight—a spot and cast approach. This can be done while wading or by working from the casting platform of a flats boat. In the latter case, elevation helps when it comes to spotting fish, and most flats boats are equipped with platforms that make poling easier and do double duty as a lookout tower. Wearing polarized glasses to enhance his ability to spot fish, the angler looks for tell-tale signs such as dorsal fins, puffs of sediment where fish are feeding, or the shadows of fish against sand bottoms.

Stealth reigns supreme in flats fishing. A poor or sloppy cast, any noise, or a host of other disturbances can spook wary fish in shallow, crystal-clear water. The ideal cast, usually fairly long, puts the fly well in front of fish and strips it in front of them as they move or as the fly is stripped. The ability to make lengthy casts without a lot of false casting, and to shoot appreciable amounts of line, is important.

Most flats fishing is done using streamers, but surface poppers work on species such as barracuda and redfish. Sound, functional tackle is essential. Long, powerful runs, even by bonefish

**below** There are several possibilities in fishing saltwater. You can fish from shore, from a dock or pier, and from a boat. The species you are likely to attract will vary accordingly.

weighing only three or four pounds, are common, while a tarpon or a powerful redfish can literally tire you out in a fight lasting a half hour or more.

There are many techniques and pieces of equipment applicable to saltwater fishing. In the main, although sea trout and puppy drum (smaller redfish) might be exceptions, saltwater fishing appeals to the more advanced angler.

## billfish
Any saltwater fish capable of being caught on standard tackle can be taken on a fly rod. This even includes billfish, with sailfish and marlin being taken by anglers using powerful 12-weight (or larger) rods equipped with shooting-head, fast-sinking lines. Teasers are often used to attract billfish, but the final hookup comes with flies tied on hooks honed to razor sharpness and attached to 80- or 100-pound test shock tippets. This is the epitome of "big game" fly fishing, with billfish as the ultimate quarry.

## other saltwater species
There are plenty of "lesser" saltwater species that can provide real fun. They include snappers, jack crevalle, snook, dolphin (dorado), and dozens of other common and exotic species.

**above** Flats fishing can be done by wading or from a boat, for many different species. Bonefish are found in shallows, often less than 12 inches (30cm) deep.

# glossary

**arbor**
The internal or center part of the reel around which the line winds.

**attractor flies**
Patterns that do not resemble a specific insect but that are "buggy" or bright in appearance and designed to draw the attention of fish.

**backing**
Thin, strong line, usually nylon, that attaches to the fly line and allows more distance for runs from powerful fish.

**bimini twist knot**
A special knot used in saltwater fly fishing.

**blanks**
The sections or pieces from which a fly rod is constructed.

**blood knot**
A knot used to link two pieces of monofilament.

**butt**
The base or bottom end of a fly rod. Larger weight rods often feature a knob known as a fighting butt, usually made from cork.

**creel**
A device for carrying fish, usually made of wicker or canvas.

**drag**
An adjustable tension device on the fly reel that controls the amount of pressure it takes to pull line from the reel.

**duncan loop**
Also known as a uni-knot, this knot is used to attach line or backing to the reel arbor.

**ferrules**
The joints or sleeves where sections of a fly rod are united.

**floatants**
Applications (usually a powder or in solid form) used to make dry flies more buoyant and less likely to sink.

**grip**
The handle by which a fly rod is held for casting.

**guides**
Round or snake-shaped pieces of metal fixed along the length of the fly rod to hold the fly line in place.

**hemostat**
A tweezers-like device used to remove the hook from the mouths of fish.

**improved clinch knot**
Often called a fisherman's knot, this is a commonly used knot for attaching the fly to the tippet.

**keeper guide**
A guide at the base of the fly rod for holding the fly in place when you are not casting or using the rod.

**leader**
The terminal portion of fly-fishing tackle; normally made of monofilament.

**mounting**
The act of joining the various sections of a rod together.

**nail knot**
A knot used to tie the leader to the line.

**reel seat**
The portion of the rod immediately below the grip where the reel is positioned and held in place.

**reel spool**
The removable part of the reel that holds the line and contains the drag system (see above).

**roll cast**
A special cast that does not require putting the line in the air behind the fisherman.

**sproat hook**
A special design of hook often used in flies for shad.

**strike**
A term used to describe a fish hitting or taking a fly.

**strike indicator**
A device, sometimes made of brightly colored fabric, other times of foam or cork, attached to the leader for use with nymphs.

**tag**
A word used to describe the end of a piece of line or leader.

**tailwaters**
The flow of a stream below a dam.

**tapered line**
A line that changes or tapers in size with the idea of making it function better in casting. There are a number of different types of tapers.

**tippet**
The end of the leader to which the fly is tied. Often the term is used to describe a separate piece of monofilament attached to the main leader.

**turle knot**
A knot used to attach the fly to the tippet.

# index

## acknowledgments

Special thanks to Orvis London for supplying the clothing and equipment photographed in this book. Orvis London, 36A Dover Street, London W1S 4NH. With thanks to Katerina Trajkovska and Mark Anderson. Illustrations on pp. 21, 42, 43, 44, 45, 46, 47, 50 by John Woodcock

Photographs on pp. 40/41, 51, 54/55, 65, 75, 79l, 80r, 85, 86/87, 92, 93 courtesy of The Orvis Co Inc.
p. 78r Karl Weatherly/Getty Images; p. 79r Wolfgang Pölzer/Alamy; pp. 80r and 81 Alaska Stock LLC/Alamy; p. 82 Robert Holland/Getty Images